Exotiquarium

Exotiquarium

Album Art from the Space Age

jennifer mcknight-trontz

richard reddig, Contributor

 St. Martin's Griffin ♒ New York

EXOTIQUARIUM. Copyright © 1999 by Jennifer McKnight-Trontz. All rights reserved. Printed in Singapore. No part of this book may be used or reproduced in any manner whatsoever without written permission except in the case of brief quotations embodied in critical articles or reviews. For information, address St. Martin's Press, 175 Fifth Avenue, New York, N.Y. 10010

Copyright Acknowledgments

Album cover art appearing on the pages listed below has been reproduced by kind permission of the following companies:

Courtesy of Universal Music Group: pp. vi, ix, 2, 8, 17, 18, 19, 25, 31, 51, 52, 53, 63, 64, 70, 81, 84, 88, 93, 104
Courtesy of Decca Record Company Limited: pp. 29, 34
Used Courtesy of The RCA Records Label, A Unit of BMG Entertainment: pp. 9, 31, 32, 33, 53, 56, 58, 66, 74, 83, 86, 96, 100, 102
Courtesy of EMI-Capitol Entertainment Properties: pp. x, 7, 28. 38, 40, 42, 68, 70, 77, 81
Courtesy of Madacy Entertainment Group, Inc.: pp. 36, 37, 46
Courtesy of Columbia Records: pp. 20, 22, 24, 27, 30, 54, 62
Courtesy of the Welk Music Group: pp. 90, 93
Courtesy of Mercury Records: pp. 5, 12, 27, 44, 63, 80, 84, 98
Courtesy of Warner Bros. Records: pp. 3, 82, 102
Courtesy of HiFi/Rykodisc USA Shetland Park, 27 Congress Street, Salem, MA 01970: pp. 4, 41, 46, 101
Courtesy of Astralwerks: pp. 114

All quotes are from album liner notes unless noted otherwise.

Text and book design by Jennifer McKnight-Trontz
Moniker Books, Inc.
Record collection and additional research by Richard Reddig

Library of Congress Cataloging-in-Publication Data

McKnight-Trontz, Jennifer.
   Exotiquarium : album art from the space age / Jennifer McKnight-Trontz ; foreword by Lenny Dee.
     p. cm.
   Includes index.
   ISBN 0-312-20133-8
   1. Sound recordings—Album covers—United States—History—20th century. I. Title.
NC1883.U6M37 1999
741.6'6—dc21   98-41878
                                                              CIP

First St. Martin's Griffin Edition: July 1999

Contents

- Foreword Lenny Dee vii
- Introduction: The Lp and New Frontiers 1
- Music for Gracious Living 21
- Exotica 39
- The Latin Invasion 55
- The Exotic East 67
- Music for Sipping Martinis 75
- The Sounds of Space 87
- And Then There Was Stereo 95
- The Artists 104
- Discography 107
- Selected Bibliography 112
- Record-Ordering Information 115
- Acknowledgments 16
- Index 117
- Album Covers Index 118

Down South
Lenny Dee
Decca Records,
late 1950s

Foreword

Lenny Dee

What has twenty feet and six teeth? Give up? The front row at a Lenny Dee concert. It's true. Most of my fans have been my fans for forty years or more. Without their loyalty, I would not have achieved anything, and anyway, my older fans are the ones that are the most fun to play for. Still, I was surprised and pleased to learn that young people not even born in the 1950s when I began recording are listening to my music.

My converts are a little hard to find, I know, since nowadays they're only in or near St. Petersburg. That's Florida, not Russia. But back in the 1950s and 1960s I played all over the U.S. I was playing in a nightclub in Nashville in 1951 when Eddy Arnold, Red Foley, Paul Cohen, and Owen Bradley came in and heard something in my music they liked.

Decca signed me and I began working with Owen Bradley, the best A&R man ever. He started me with a backup group. We were Lenny Dee and the Dee Men. We played mostly country music during that time.

Then in 1954, Mr. Bradley asked me to make the choice of what I wanted to record.

I wrote "Plantation Boogie" and we recorded it and had a number one hit in 1955. From then on Decca expanded my repertoire. From the 1950s to the 1970s I made fifty-six albums for Decca and MCA.

I always had a wonderful relationship with my recording companies. My only real criticism was some of the album covers, especially the psychedelic ones of the 1960s and 1970s.

We had a lot of fun photographing some of the earlier covers. One of my favorites is *Down South*. We had it photographed at Cypress Gardens waterskiing park in Florida. We wanted to do a waterskiing shot of me playing the organ. Hammond kindly sent us a shell of an organ, which we placed on a small towing platform behind the boat. I sat down like I was playing, and put Miss Muffet, my toy poodle, on the top of the organ. The boat took off with me, the organ, and Miss Muffet on the back. We were going about thirty knots when the skier went by and the photo was taken. I had to change into dry clothes a few times.

I don't know if my album covers helped sell records, but I do know that my records helped sell a lot of players at Montgomery Ward. A salesman once told me my records sold more hi-fi equipment that any of their other sales tools.

I suppose my music stretched the equipment out and showed off what it could do. That makes sense, because that's how I played the organ—stretching it out and showing it off.

From the beginning my music was unique. I played the accordion before I played the organ, but when I heard the organ playing of Tommy Ott and Milt Herth I was excited by it. I then heard music and sounds in my head that I wanted to try to create on the organ. When I got out of the Navy after World War II, my father bought me a Hammond Model A that had been made in 1933. I recorded and performed with that Hammond until about 1970, when I began playing a Hammond B 3000.

The organ allowed me to express my emotions. The music I made, the music we were all making, brought people together. People danced a lot. You could feel the love in the music then, and really hear it in your heart.

There were so many new sounds to explore, like electrified instruments and multitrack recording.

It was a creative time and, for me, and I think most of us, a happy time. Just listen to the music, look at the album covers. You can hear and see all the fun we had.

Many of Dee's album covers featured Dee in silly poses and often took advantage of Dee's name with such titles as Mellow-Dee, Hi-Dee-Fi, Dee-Most, Dee-Licious, and Dee-Lirious.

Dee-Lirious:
Hi-Fi Organ Solos
with a Beat
Lenny Dee
Decca Records, 1956

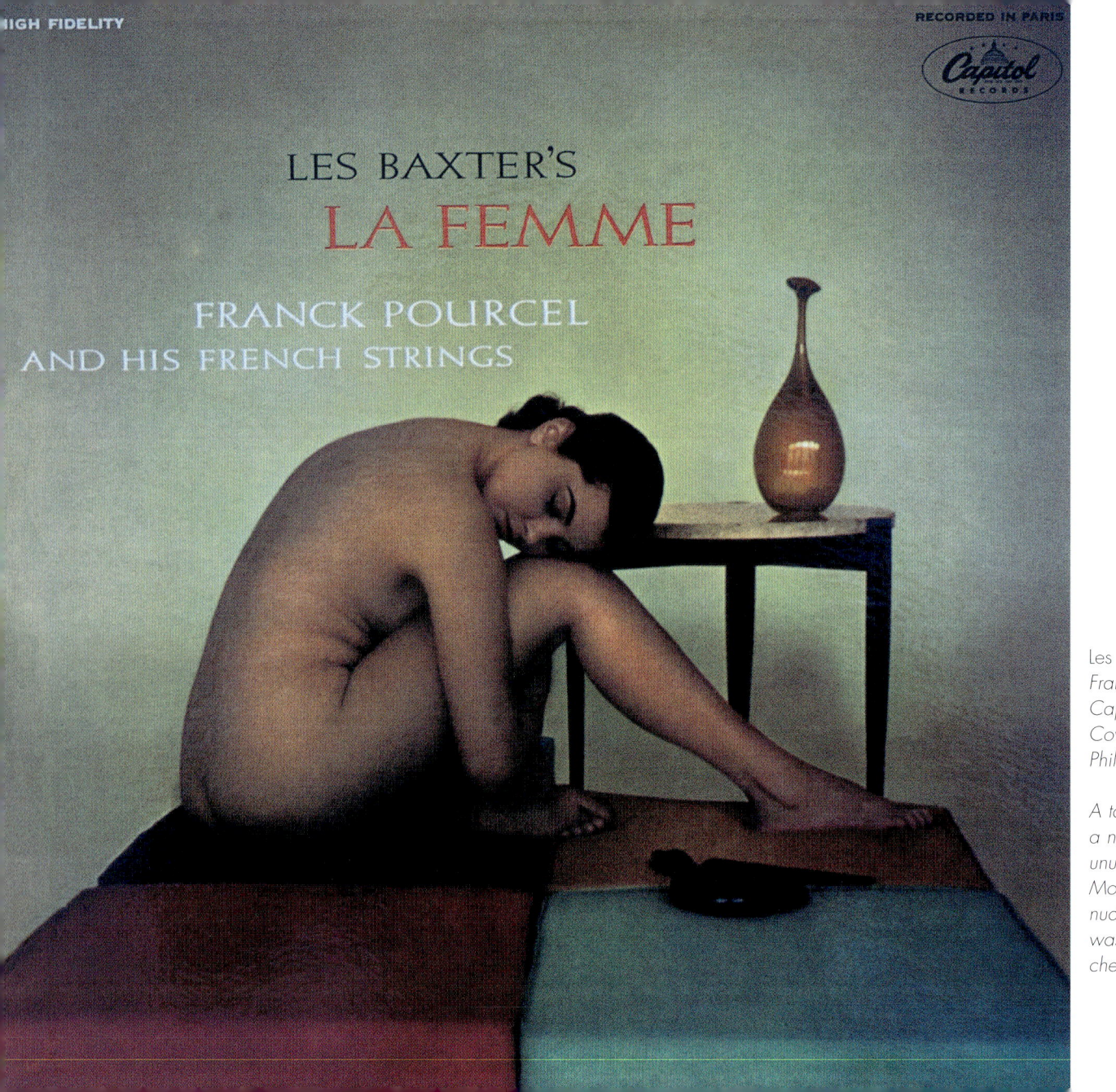

Les Baxter's La Femme
Franck Pourcel
Capitol Records, 1957
Cover photo:
Phillip March

A tasteful color photo of a nude woman was unusual in the 1950s. Most of the nude or semi-nude album cover art was of the cheesecake variety.

Introduction:

The LP and New Frontiers

Digging through thrift stores and used-record shops, vinyl archaeologists discovered an entire lost culture in the dusty heaps of discarded musical has-beens. Buried beneath Barry Manilow and Shaun Cassidy were Technicolor images of erupting volcanoes, voluptuous women, space cosmonauts, and cocktail-sipping couples.

A cover alone was worth the pocket change.

These disavowed remnants are colorful glimpses into the 1950s and 1960s—an era obsessed with technological advancements and new frontiers. The covers depict the good life—tropical island vacations, sexy women, well-paying jobs, happy families, comfortable homes, and cocktail parties.

Space Age Pop is the musical interpretation of these dreams. It comprises the eerie, mesmerizing sounds of Mood music; the Polynesian, Hawaiian, Caribbean, and jungle melodies of Exotica; the hi-fidelity and stereo-inspired sounds of bachelor pad music; and the dreamy, seductive rhapsodies of cocktail tunes.

After Dinner Music
Victor Young
Decca Records, 1956

The scenes on these pages are the most common images presented on covers in the 1950s and 1960s: sultry and sexy, and sweet and old-fashioned.

Space Age Pop captivated sophisticated record buyers of the Eisenhower and Kennedy years. Ideas were flourishing, and technology provided a means for spreading them. Television, records, and film became accessible to most Americans in unprecedented ways.

The Golden Age of vinyl began in 1948 when Columbia introduced "a revolutionary new product"—the long-playing record. Before LPs, records came in a box set with one or two songs per side. The new 33⅓-rpm microgroove ten-inch LPs (twelve-inch would soon become the standard) had a playing time of twenty-three minutes per side and could include ten to twelve songs per record. Music lovers no longer needed radio for continuous play.

A year after Columbia unveiled the LP, the label's sales were 3.5 million—phenomenal for the time. In 1949 Capitol, RCA, and Decca all went over to the new speed, and then RCA introduced the seven-inch 45-rpm single.

Made of a new plastic called Vinylite, the records sounded better and did not scratch as easily as the 78s, which were made of shellac. The stronger Vinylite could hold more grooves per inch without cracking; hence the name "microgroove."

Not everyone was pleased with the new technology, mainly because it meant buying a new turntable. But the new equipment also produced higher-fidelity sounds.

Serious music lovers praised the records. Soon, the recording industry predicted, the rest of America would follow. And they were right. By the late 1950s vinyl had basically replaced the shellac.

Hi-fidelity—and later stereophonic music—became a requirement for the good life. The comfortable home included a library of records for every mood. One of the leading labels in recording standards, Audio Fidelity, offered this advice on many of its records, including *Tropical Cruise:* "Although any 33⅓ RPM record playing equipment may be used in playing this recording, it is recommended that playback equipment of extreme wide range and fidelity be used so that the recordings may be enjoyed to their utmost."

In the 1950s, American homes, especially in the new suburbia, became full-service temples with new appliances, television, a state-of-the-art sound system, and the music you wanted anytime you wanted it. A simple LP could put your life in order (such as Columbia's *Music for Gracious Living* series), help you relax, even make you feel good. Why leave home?

Teenagers danced to singles of Bill Haley and the Comets, while adults relaxed to the mood melodies of Paul Weston, the Melachrino Strings, and Mantovani. Heavenly, cascading strings proved perfect background music. This was the stuff for grown-ups.

It wasn't long before these respectable string-enhanced melodies were taken over by wild, intriguing, exotic sounds. "Smoke Gets in Your Eyes" became "Smoke Gets in Your Eyes Cha-Cha-Cha." Often these new songs included animal noises, foreign instruments, and "extraterrestrial" sounds. Alien and primitive cultures could be channeled into your living room through music. This was Exotica.

Exotic motifs arrived in America with World War II veterans who were hypnotized by what they had seen in the South Pacific. By the early 1950s Polynesia had settled in the suburbs. Restaurants, bowling alleys, and bars were transformed into glorified tiki huts. Music from Africa, Europe, the Orient, the Middle East, and Latin America followed.

Exotica's explorer extraordinaire, Les Baxter,

Mind If I Make Love to You
The Sensuous Music of
Pete King
*Warner Bros. Records,
1959*

Taboo
Arthur Lyman
HiFi Records, 1958
Photo: Werner Stoy

"safaried" around the world in search of new sounds. His albums present a glimpse of what he learned: *Ritual of the Savage, African Jazz,* and *Jungle Jazz.* Baxter, along with Yma Sumac, Martin Denny, and other Exoticists, delivered hefty helpings of taboo to suburbanite living rooms, offering Americans a window on their primal urges.

A sophisticated cocktail party might have included the records of comedian Jackie Gleason. *Music for Lovers Only; Music, Martinis, and Memories;* and *Oooo!* provided a sentimental, romantic background party-goers could chat over. After a few rounds, the hostess would invariably put on the latest dance record, and before anyone could say "Mambo," they were out on the floor vigorously moving their hips.

Hi-fidelity traveled easily into the new Space Age, when the moon was America's national frontier. Labels released numerous space records in time with such movies as *Forbidden Planet, War of the Worlds,* and the lovably awful Ed Wood film *Plan 9 from Outer Space.*

On *Soundproof* (1956), piano duo Ferrante and Teicher present a collection of "the most unusual, massive, and baffle-busting arrangements ever recorded." Sid Bass begins his selections on *From Another World* (1956) with a spaceship launch. The liner notes boast that the music "couldn't be played by a 'live' orchestra without the aid of a tape recorder behind the scenes. And even though this is 'universeal' music, it just can't be played—at least not by Earth-type musicians."

For Space Age Pop musicians, the studio, lounge, or tiki palace was their stage. These gentlemen (99 percent men) were comfortable in the corporate confines of the record labels or the respectable adult venues. Their talent lay in arrang-

The Cat's Meow
Jerry Murad's Harmonicats
Mercury Records,
late 1950s

ing, conducting, and performing, but rarely in songwriting. For a while it seemed as though songs were not being written, merely rearranged.

After "Caravan," "Misirlou," and "Hawaiian War Chant" had been covered sufficiently, music listeners and musicians themselves began to tire of ukuleles and Chinese gongs.

In the late 1950s a new creation called stereo thrust the music back in motion. The labels championed stereo with terms like "Spectra-sonic" and "Visual Sound." RCA's *Stereo Action* series brought listeners "unmatched fidelity through the full sound spectrum, plus the exciting new illusion of sound in motion. Soloists and entire sections of the orchestra appear to move thrillingly back and forth across the room."

The studio became a high-tech recording lab. Musicians, arrangers, and engineers worked diligently to create outrageously percussive and "electrified" harmonies. Ferrante and Teicher and harpist Robert Maxwell launched otherwise ordinary instruments into orbit.

Percussion became a popular vehicle for showcasing stereo's capabilities. While the labels tripped over themselves promoting stereo, musicians tripped over their numerous percussion instruments. On his 1950s and 1960s albums *Persuasive Percussion* and *Provocative Percussion*, Enoch Light convinced the last few monaural anachronists that stereo was it. The series featured such "oldies" as "April in Portugal" and "Song of India" played with a concentrated dose of percussion. Light believed music should be actively listened to, not played in the background, and his liner notes went into brain-numbing detail describing which effects to listen for in each song. He was only one of many stereo-mongers.

For the 1962 album *Latin-Esque*, Juan Garcia Esquivel took great measures to ensure the purest separation of channels — dividing his orchestra in half and even positioning each in separate buildings.

Space Age Pop developed out of America's insatiable appetite for the new and improved, providing grown-ups with the music they wanted: seductive moods, primitive beats, and fantastic effects. The music flourished from the early 1950s into the mid 1960s, then disappeared when politics invaded culture and lyrics took over the medium. Space Age Pop would end the way it started, on the edge of war.

Primitiva
Martin Denny
Liberty Records, 1958
Photo: Garrett-Howard
Cover design: Bill Pate

Instruments employed:
Japanese Koto
Prayer bells
African thumpiano
Tuned chromatic
   marimbula
Primitive log from
   New Guinea
Burmese gongs
Burmese cymbals
Japanese glass chimes
Bamboo chimes
Tuned steel drum
Cuzoo

Blast Off!
Ferrante and Teicher
ABC Paramount,
late 1950s
Cover art:
Viceroy/Zwillinger

Other Worlds Other Sounds
Esquivel and His Orchestra
RCA Victor, 1958

The Concept Album

A concept album is a collection of songs tied together by a theme.

The Beatles' 1969 *Sgt. Pepper's Lonely Heart's Club Band* is often cited as the first concept album. But Space Age Pop artists were recording them as soon as the LP came out in the late 1940s.

Les Baxter's 1952 album *Ritual of the Savage* is a tone poem of "the sound and struggle of the jungle."

Baxter's compositions take the listener on a virtual safari through Africa—from "Busy Port" to "The Ritual."

Melachrino's mood series (*Music for Dining, Music for Relaxation,* and so on) included songs conducive to a certain chosen experience.

Some Space Age Pop concept albums revolved around abstract themes: Jackie Gleason's *Music for* series was built around emotions. His first, *Music for Lovers Only*, contained songs such as "My Funny Valentine" and "I'm in the Mood for Love" chosen for "lovers only": "In this album Jackie Gleason has chosen a group of love's most appealing melodies…tender ballads that have special significance for all of us. Here is tuneful, sentimental music for your most relaxed listening moments."

In the late 1950s Command Records' founder, Enoch Light, invented an essential component to the concept album—the gatefold.

The gatefold is the opening fold that allows the album to open like a book—allocating more room to explain the concept of the album.

The Songs

Exotica and Space Age Pop artists relied on a standard repertoire of songs. They included remnants of the big band era and exotic numbers by artists such as Les Baxter and Cuban songwriter Ernesto Lecuona. Some are romantic and nostalgic, others foreign and primitive. If any of the following are on a record, it's definitely worth considering.

April In Portugal
(Raul Farrao) *Lisbon in Twilight*, George Melachrino; *Four Corners of the World*, Esquivel

Autumn Leaves
(Joseph Kosma) *Sea of Dreams*, Nelson Riddle; *Autumn Leaves*, Roger Williams

Babalu
(Ernesto and Margarita Lecuona) *Exotic Percussion*, Stanley Black

Bali Ha'i
South Pacific, Percy Faith; *High Fi and Wide*, The Three Suns; *Far Away Places*, Enoch Light; *Lure of Paradise*, André Kostelanetz

The Breeze and I
(Ernesto Lecuona) *Pianos in Paradise*, Ferrante and Teicher; *Music for Playboys to Play By*, The Hollywood Playboys Orchestra; *Caribbean Moonlight*, Les Baxter

Caravan
(Juan Tizol and Duke Ellington) *Candido in Indigo*, Candido; *Dee-Lirous*, Lenny Dee; *Brass and Bamboo*, Tak Shindo; *Fantastic Percussion!*, Felix Slatkin; *Jungle Drums*, Morton Gould

Ebb Tide
(Music, Robert Maxwell) *Taboo Vol. 2*, Arthur Lyman; *Lotus Land*, Gene Rains

Hawaiian War Chant
(Johnny Noble and Leoleohako) *Red Sails in the Sunset*, Johnny Lei Orchestra; *Captivation*, The Outriggers; *Hawaiian Percussion*, Billy Mure

Hawaiian Wedding Song
(Al Hoffman, Dick Manning) *Hawaii Tattoo*, Martin Denny; *The 50th State*, Charles Bud Dant

In a Persian Market
(Albert Ketelbey) *High Fi and Wide*, The Three Suns; *East of Suez*, 101 Strings

Misirlou
(Nicholas Roubanis) *Taboo*, Arthur Lyman; *Exotic Percussion*, Stanley Black; *Wild Percussion and Horns a' Plenty*, Dick Schory

Moon of Manakoora
(Alfred Newman) *Jasmine and Jade*, Axel Stordahl; *Music of the Islands*, The Mauna Loa Islanders; *Lure of Paradise*, André Kostelanetz

The Peanut Vendor
(Moises Simon) *Latin Fever*, Jack Costanzo

Perdido
(Juan Tizol) *Bongos from the South*, Edmundo Ros

Quiet Village
(Les Baxter) *The Ritual of the Savage*, Les Baxter; *Exotica*, Martin Denny; *Bahia*, Arthur Lyman

Red Sails in the Sunset
(Hugh Williams) *Hawaiian Tattoo*, Martin Denny

Siboney
(Ernesto Lecuona) *Carnival Tropicana*, André Kostelanetz; *Malaguena*, Percy Faith

Taboo
(Ernesto and Margarita Lecuona) *Bongos from the South*, Edmundo Ros; *Taboo*, Arthur Lyman; *Pianos in Paradise*, Ferrante and Teicher

Let's Dance
David Carroll
Mercury Records,
mid-1950s

In the spirit of Muzak and artistic license, Exotica and Space Age Pop artists took some unsuspecting songs and made them all their own.

Hang On Sloopy
The Shadow of Your Smile, Arthur Lyman

Incense and Peppermints
A Taste of India, Martin Denny

Fever
Fever & Smoke, The Three Suns

Midnight Cowboy
Exotic Moog, Martin Denny

Lay Lady Lay
Ferrante and Teicher

S'wanee River
Dynamic Dimension, Henri René

Lullaby of Birdland
'S Awful Nice, Ray Conniff

The A & R Men

In the 1950s Artists & Repertoire men (99 percent men) decided all of the hows, whats, whos, and whens of the record business.

These A&R executives bought songs from publishers or commissioned them from composers, then decided who would record the material. They also were in the studio working on sessions with recording engineers.
In the mid-1960s the popularity of more independent-minded performers, such as the Beatles, helped transfer power to the musicians and songwriters.

Some A&R men also recorded their own music, including Space Age Pop artists Percy Faith, Mitch Miller, Paul Weston, and Hugo Winterhalter.

Other Space Age Pop artists who were A&R executives or staff composers and arrangers included: Gordon Jenkins at Decca; Henri René, Leo Addeo, Marty Gold, and Hugo Winterhalter at RCA; Bert Kaempfert at Polydor; Percy Faith, Paul Weston, and Mitch Miller at Columbia; Les Baxter and Pete Rugolo at Capitol; and Richard Haymen and David Carroll at Mercury.

Sing Along with Mitch

Mitch Miller was Columbia's chief A&R executive. He was a huge influence on music in the 1950s, especially easy-listening. He oversaw the careers of Guy Mitchell, Percy Faith, and André Kostelanetz.

Miller chose to ignore rock. Instead, he succeeded with his own series of albums entitled *Sing Along with Mitch*. The idea sparked seventeen more LPs by 1963.

His first, *Sing Along with Mitch*, in 1958 included "That Old Gang of Mine," "Till We Meet Again," and "Down by the Old Mill Stream." By 1962 Columbia had sold a million copies of the record. He followed with more: *More Sing Along with Mitch, Still More Sing Along with Mitch, Party Sing Along with Mitch, Folk Songs Sing Along with Mitch, Fireside Sing Along with Mitch, Saturday Night Sing Along with Mitch, Sentimental Sing Along with Mitch,* and *Memories Sing Along with Mitch*. Eager to show the world his face, Miller was always a good sport for the album covers. He even donned a silly Santa hat for *Christmas Sing Along with Mitch*.

The Covers

During the early years of the phonographic record, most covers were of a thick, drab-colored paste-board. The artist's name and the record title were stamped on the front and spine. These "tombstones," as they were commonly called, were usually displayed spine out on store shelves. There was no need for elaborate covers.

This all changed in 1938 when Columbia Records designer Alex Steinweiss created the first illustrated cover: A Rogers and Hart collection. After a few more, the Steinweiss covers dramatically increased sales for Columbia. *Newsweek* reported that Steinweiss's package for Bruno Walter's Beethoven *Eroica* symphony outsold the same release, in an unillustrated package, by 895 percent. The "tombstones" were as good as dead.

Steinweiss's covers were distinguished by their curlicue "Steinweiss Scrawl" lettering and the flat, colorful style reminiscent of European poster artist Joseph Binder, with whom he had worked before Columbia. Later Steinweiss invented the paperboard 33⅓ LP cover for Columbia, the standard until compact discs.

By the 1950s photography replaced illustration as the medium of choice. Designers found more power in a simple, bold photograph and little copy.

As the recording industry grew, each label began to develop its own visual style to convey the mood of the music and attract buyers. New York–based RCA and Columbia favored elegant, sophisticated presentations, while Hollywood's Capitol preferred a more exotic approach to cover art. All heeded general market research, which told them to tap the seemingly contradictory principles of security and sex.

Family Listening

Labels appealed to America's need for security with music for the entire family and "quiet evenings at home." "Family" series such as RCA's *Moods in Music* and Columbia's *Music for Gracious Living* profiled the perfect and busy American family. The cover artists took cues from TV and movie families of matching furniture, attractive friends, and well-behaved children.

The Audiophile

Labels used technology to attract their most loyal buyers — the audiophiles. These were, as Los Angeles cartoonist and Space Age Pop aficionado Byron Werner surmised, "lonely guys with too much disposable income who are nitpicky about their stereos."
The true audiophile needed little prodding. A few technological graphs and charts were enough to open his wallet. These albums often featured geometric shapes and patterns to mimic the movement of the music.

Sex and the Single Man

The man who had a life—the Space Age bachelor—wanted more than technology. He wanted ambience and the power to seduce. "Cheesecake" covers featured scantily dressed women of all shapes and sizes lounging in martini glasses, erupting from volcanoes, caressing instruments, and straddling stuffed animals. Sexual innuendo, double entendres, and sometimes blatant requests spoke from the shelves: *Mmm Nice, I'm in the Mood for Love,* and *Let's Make Love* were hard to resist.

Travelogues

For travelogue LPs—records that included songs about a place—exotic locale photography was frequently used. Often a "native girl" was superimposed onto the photograph.

Many photos were courtesy of airlines. In the time surrounding Hawaii's induction into the U.S., Americans were visiting Hawaii and the Polynesian Islands in record numbers. Perhaps the "authentic" island music had inspired them.

Unfortunately, for marketing purposes, ethnic and cultural accuracy were ignored. Sometimes the place in the photo was miles away from the music. Golden Tone's *Hawaiian Holiday* features a photo "courtesy of British West Indies Airways."

But the studios should get credit for going to great lengths to dress the models in native costumes. In this respect they were devoted to cultural accuracy—and if the costume was too tight, they put her on the cover anyway.

The Models

A top-echelon artist's photo could sell a record by itself.

There were only a few well-known Space Age Pop artists famous and good-looking enough to sell their records. They included Roger Williams, Perez Prado, Ray Anthony, Louis Prima, and Yma Sumac. Les Baxter and Esquivel made an occasional appearance, as did Percy Faith and Xavier Cugat.

But usually they let a model sell the album.

Often these models were unrecognizable from album to album—in evening wear on one and jungle rags on the next.

Martin Denny often used model and aspiring singer Sandy Warner. She appeared on his first album, *Exotica*, and enough of the others to be called the "Exotica girl."

Cugat was famous for featuring his current woman. Wife number three (he had four), cocktail songstress Abbe Lane, often appeared on the covers of his Mercury recordings of the 1950s.

Tabu
Ralph Font and His Orchestra
Westminster, late 1950s

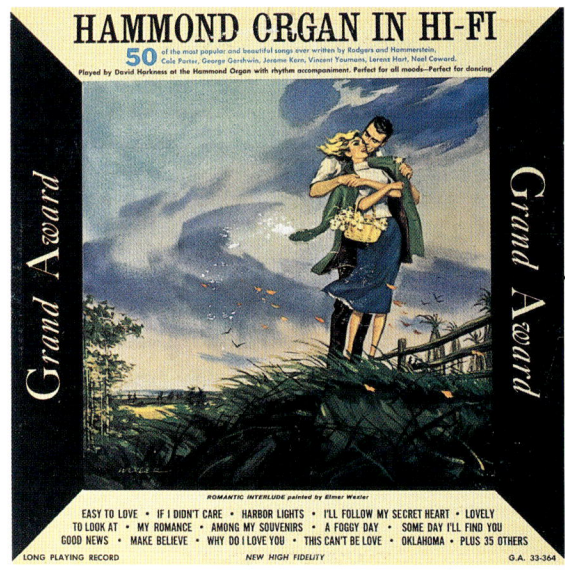

Hammond Organ in Hi-Fi
David Harkness
Grand Award Records, mid-1950s
Cover painting: Elmer Wexler

Provocative Percussion
Enoch Light and the Light Brigade
Command Records, 1959
Cover art: Josef Albers

Guitar Underground
*Enoch Light
Project 3, 1966
Cover art: Charles Murphy*

The Light Covers

Enoch Light's career spanned the three record labels he founded: The early 1950s with Grand Award, the late 1950s with Command, and the 1960s and 1970s with Project 3. The labels reflected the continuous change in popular music and album cover design.

For Grand Award covers, Light often chose the work of amateur painters. His next project, Command, featured bold, abstract images, many by artist Joseph Albers. Like the percussion on the record, these covers boinged and bounced.

Many Project 3 covers illustrated the eventual transition to the 1960s album cover art of psychedelic colors and images. Clearly, Light was prepared for the next generation.

Music for Gracious Living
Do-It-Yourself
Peter Barclay and His Orchestra
Columbia Records, 1955
Photo: Hedrich-Blessing

Music for Gracious Living

An important part of gracious living is certainly the joy of gracious entertaining. Consideration for the tastes of one's guest is as important as a smile or a handshake.

—Foursome, *Music for Gracious Living Series*

In the 1950s America's leisure habits changed forever. Gone were the Rockwellesque family gatherings around the radio.

The LP and television proved irresistible, shiny new substitutes.

Mood music took advantage of the record's new long-playing time, and capitalized on America's hectic lifestyle to reach a level of popularity it had not seen before, and has not seen since.

Purveyors of this Mood, or "easy-listening" music promised to provide soothing, comforting melodies that the new America wanted in those stressful times. With LPs, you could go about your daily business without having to turn the record over every few minutes. You could get into a mood and stay there.

Dream Time Music by Paul Weston
Paul Weston
Columbia Records, early 1950s

Paul Weston initiated the Mood frenzy in 1945 with *Music for Dreaming*. "Mature" record buyers were captivated by his rich, smooth, and romantic melodies. The record sold an impressive 175,000 copies.

Weston followed with several *Music for* albums, including *Music for Memories*, *Music for Reflection*, and *Music for Romance*.

The recording industry began to recognize the enormous desire for easy listening.

Soundtracks to Family Living

To appeal to the family unit, labels released series of Mood records tailored for busy American homes.

Columbia's first, *Quiet Music*, recorded in the early 1950s, was a collection of instrumentals performed by the Columbia Salon Orchestra. *Volume I* included "flowing melodies of yesterday" like "Clair de Lune," "La Paloma," and Schubert's "Serenade." Other records included *Volume V: A Marek Weber Musicale* and *Volume VI: Relaxing with Cugat*.

Columbia's greatest contribution to the general welfare was in 1955 with a series called *Music for Gracious Living*. Albums included *Barbecue*, *Foursome*, *Buffet*, *After the Dance*, and a guide to home improvement, *Do-It-Yourself*.

On *Do-It-Yourself*, Peter Barclay and His Orchestra perform such task-inspiring melodies as "The Stars Will Remember" and "Forever and Ever." The liner notes offer endearing tips for making your home more comfortable: "In every modern home there should be a music room, devoted to the enjoyment of Columbia's superb radio, phonograph, and television equipment."

"You can convert your table-model television set into a handsome console. It will put your screen at correct viewing height, too…"

The other major record labels produced their own lines of musical wallpaper. Capitol released *Background Music*, a series of four albums consisting of swing, polka, show tunes, and romantic songs.

RCA trotted out *Moods in Music* by popular British conductor George Melachrino. The collection included Melachrino's harmonic touch and string-enhanced music for dining, relaxing, daydreaming, inspiration, reading, and even studying.

Like Columbia's *Music for Gracious Living*, *Moods in Music* offered tips for becoming the kind of groomed, smart, happy people featured on the record covers: "A daydream can fly you to the uttermost exotic land, bring you the choicest of the world's luxuries, even transport you to another planet." The title, of course, was *Music for Daydreaming*.

Music for Dining recommended the correct dish to complement each song: "Too Young" should be served with pâté de foie gras and truffles; "September Song," lobster mayonnaise or vichyssoise; and "Clopin Clopant" should start out the main entrée.

During the 1950s Melachrino made more than fifty LPs for RCA.

RCA also released the twelve-volume *For Hi-Fi Living*, "specially created for your personal music programming at home." Mirrors of everyday life, such as *I Could Have Danced All Night, I Married an Angel,* and *Lazy Afternoon* were designed for modern living.

Each album boasted carefully chosen light instrumentals by such music giants as Irving Berlin, George Gershwin, and Cole Porter.

The screen door stayed open for Mercury Records, which brought home *Music to Live By*. The high-fidelity demonstration record featured popular jazz and classical excerpts to fit every mood.

As recording techniques improved, Mood and easy-listening artists pondered ways to enrich their music. They discovered that string instruments produced light sounds that were also intense.

Strings, Strings, Strings

Soon Paul Weston's dreamtime serenades gave way to super symphonies consisting of strings—scores of them.

British–Italian composer Annunzio Mantovani was the maestro of strings, and the first musician in the world to sell a million stereo LPs.

Mantovani's "cathedralized classics" appealed to "the overworked and somewhat pressured man of today's complex world…and the curious, alert listener."

Mantovani had his first major hit in 1950 with "Charmaine," a tune from the early 1900s. His "cascading strings" treatment established him as the

*Music for Gracious Living,
Foursome*
Peter Barclay and His
Orchestra
Columbia Records
Photo: Hedrich-Blessing

king of Mood music. He made fifty-one hit LPs between 1952 and 1973, and seven million-selling albums including *Immortal Classics* in 1954 and *Exodus and Other Great Themes* in 1960.

Another Brit mulling over moods was Frank Chacksfield. Chacksfield's romantic background music was also "smooth, controlled and sophisticated." His rendition of Robert Maxwell's "Ebb Tide" reached number two in the U.S. in 1953. That same year the song "Limelight" from the Charlie Chaplin film of the same name went gold.

Like Mantovani, Chacksfield specialized in renditions of waltzes, ballads, and movie themes.

The biggest string group of them all was the 101 Strings. As Joseph Lanza writes in his 1994 book *Elevator Music*, the Strings were popular for "the global aspirations of today's 'world' sound but without any pretense to ethnomusicological accuracy."

The Strings traversed the world, releasing more than two hundred albums that captured the "soul of" Israel, Spain, Mexico, England, and so forth. Listeners were delighted with their neatly packaged versions of the world.

Gypsy Campfires includes a token violin, *Hawaiian Paradise*, a ukulele, and the *Soul of Israel*, a collection of songs about and for "the peoples of this small land…[who] have known suffering down through the centuries."

The 101 Strings began in Hamburg, Germany, under director Dick L. Miller. They were advertised as "the World's First Stereo-Scored Orchestra."

The Strings' lush sound was due to the amazing number of string instruments "played by the finest musicians in Europe," and "recording techniques using specially designed microphones that could compensate for any possible distortion."

Sweet Music and Memories...
Billy Vaughn and His Orchestra
Dot Records
Cover lingerie: Vanity Fair

- André Kostelanetz was another string king. Kostelanetz first took advantage of the power of strings on his popular radio programs in the 1930s and 1940s. He and his 50 percent string orchestra sold more than fifty million high-class pop records for Columbia. *High Fidelity* called him the "prophet of the classics for the masses."

He often praised the phonograph for democratizing music and gladly pioneered the mission to bring Rachmaninoff, Verdi, and Puccini to Americans.

He also was a leader in tune with his subjects. When Latin music seduced America, he released *Lure of Spain* and *Carnival Tropicana*; when Polynesia captivated the mainland, he brought out *Lure of the Tropics* and *Lure of Paradise*.

- Another Columbia gold mine, Percy Faith, described his goal as "satisfying the millions of devotees of that pleasant American institution known as the quiet evening at home."

A guru in the popular instrumental category, Faith recorded more than eighty records and three number one hits: "Delicado" in 1952, "Theme from Moulin Rouge" in 1953, and "Theme from a Summer Place" in 1960.

He was one of the first to record a series of "Songs from" Broadway shows, including *Kismet, Lil' Abner, South Pacific, The Sound of Music,* and *Camelot*.

He yearned to record more Latin albums, like *Malaguena* and *Viva!*, which are considered two of his best. But his adoring public, and consequently Columbia, preferred his string-heavy pop and schlock.

For Your Shopping Pleasure

In the 1950s Mood music was piped into glistening department stores and new supermarkets to soften the bright lights, smooth the harsh surroundings, and perhaps subliminally open the wallet.

The king of supermarket music was Ray Conniff. His first LP, the 1956 *'S Wonderful,* was one of the best-selling instrumental albums of the time. His formula, which he had developed over years of studying the hits, was to substitute the women's voices for the trumpet section and the men's voices for the sax section. He later made the chorus bigger and brought it up front.

His method managed to both soothe and invigorate. Under the guidance of Columbia A&R chief Mitch Miller, Conniff produced twenty-five top forty records, including *'S Wonderful, 'S Marvelous*, and *'S Awful Nice*.

- Years before the synthesizer, piano duo Arthur Ferrante and Louis Teicher extracted the sounds of gongs, drums, xylophones, castanets, and harpsichords from their pianos. They achieved these sounds by inserting rubber wedges, wads of paper, and sticks into the stringbed. They even used metal bars and chains across the strings.

After several albums, they signed with United Artists in 1960 and abandoned their modification techniques for a more supermarket-style orchestral accompaniment. Subsequently, they produced eleven top one hundred hits, including the theme from *The Apartment*.

'S Awful Nice
Ray Conniff
Columbia Records,
1959

Happy Occasions
Paul Pincus and His
Orchestra
Mercury Records,
mid-1950s

The Enchanted Ferrante
and Teicher
Ferrante and Teicher
United Artists, mid-1960s

Waltzes to Remember...
Frank Chacksfield and His Orchestra
*London Records,
mid-1950s*

Lure of the Tropics
André Kostelanetz
Columbia Records, mid-1950s

Swing Low in Hi Fi
Spirituals for Orchestra
Percy Faith, mid-1950s
Columbia Records
Photo: Dan Wynn

I Married an Angel
Hill Bowen and His Orchestra
RCA Custom, 1957

That Happy Feeling
Bert Kaempfert
Decca Records,
early 1960s

Music for Dining
The Melachrino Strings
RCA Victor, mid-1950s

Music for Reading
The Melachrino Strings
RCA Victor, mid-1950s

It wasn't long before there were records *for* and *to* almost everything:

Music to Help You Stop Smoking
Music to Strip By
Music to Paint By
Music for Lovely Lovers
Music to Read James Bond By
Music for a Lonely Night
Music for Cooking with Gas
Music for Airports
Music to Read *Life's* Year End Issue By
Music to Lift Your Spirits
Music to Move By
Music for Your Plants

Music for Daydreaming
The Melachrino Strings
RCA Victor, mid-1950s

Mantovani's biggest hit songs include:
"Charmaine," 1951
"Greensleeves," 1952
"Song from Moulin Rouge"
"Swedish Rhapsody"
"Christmas Carols"
"Strauss Waltzes," all in 1953
"Lonely Ballerina," 1954
"Song Hits from Theaterland," 1955
"Film Encores," 1957
"Gems Forever," 1958

Romantic Melodies
Annunzio Mantovani
London Records,
early 1950s

The Cult of 101 Strings

Albums not to be missed:

- A Night in the Tropics
- Astounding! High Fidelity
- A Bridal Bouquet
- Honeymoon in South America
- Sugar and Spice
- Pipe Organ Favorites
- Russian Fireworks
- Rhapsody
- Italian Hits
- I Love Paris
- Symphony for Lovers
- Opera Without Words
- Broadway Cocktail Party
- Back Beat Symphony
- African Safari
- Fly Me to the Moon
- The Blues
- Songs of England
- Soul of Israel
- Award Winning Scores from the Silver Screen
- The Glory of Christmas
- Concerto Under the Stars
- Soul of Spain
- A Mediterranean Cruise to the Rivieras, Spain, France and Italy
- Hit American Waltzes
- Quiet Hours
- Grand Canyon Suite
- Soul of Mexico
- Songs of the Seasons in Japan
- Fire and Romance of South America
- Americana
- A Romantic Mood for Dining and Dreaming
- The Soul of the Gypsies
- The Jet Set
- Astro Sounds

The 101 Strings Play the Best American Waltzes
101 Strings
Somerset Records,
late 1950s

East of Suez
101 Strings
Somerset Records,
late 1950s

Gypsy Campfires
101 Strings
*Somerset Records,
late 1950s*

Sugar and Spice
101 Strings
*Somerset Records,
late 1950s*

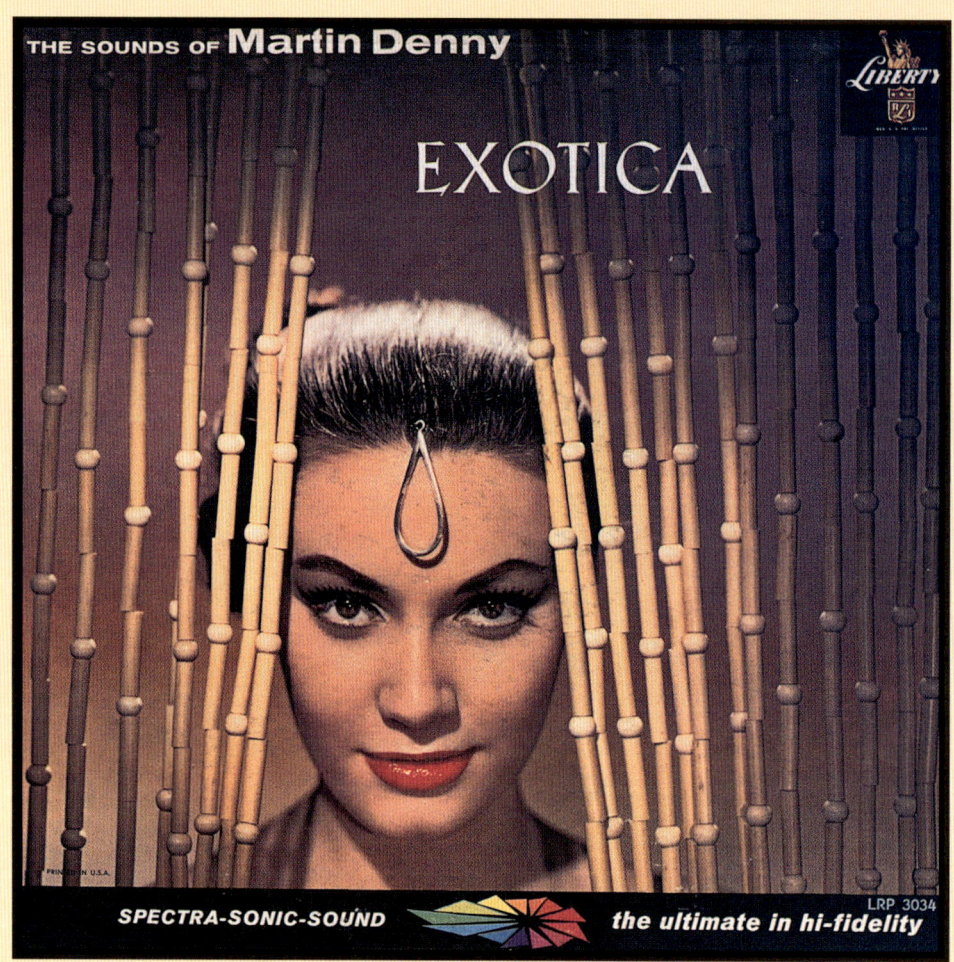

Primordial Exotica
Some of the first Exotica appeared in the 1920s during Duke Ellington's jungle period, including the songs "Creole Love Call," and "Caravan."

Exotica
Martin Denny
Liberty Records, 1957
Model: Sandy Warner
Photo: Garrett-Howard

Exotica

While Melachrino and Mantovani mastered string-laden background music, Les Baxter, Martin Denny, and Arthur Lyman experimented with a provocative new strain of Mood music called Exotica.

Jungle Exotica

Baxter introduced Jungle Exotica in 1951 with *Ritual of the Savage*—"A tone poem of the sound and struggle of the jungle." As with other albums of the genre, the music had more in common with, say, Tarzan movies than the Congo.

On the album, Baxter blends "ritualistic melodies and seductive rhythms of the natives of distant jungles and tropical ports to capture all the color and fervor so expressive of the emotions of these people."

The album embarks at "Busy Port," takes a ride on "A Jungle River Boat," visits

Baxter's best:
Music out of the Moon
The Passions
Tamboo!
Caribbean Moonlight
Skins!
Space Escapade
The Sacred Idol
Jewels of the Sea
Barbarian

Ritual of the Savage
Les Baxter
Capitol Records, 1952
Cover art:
William George

"Quiet Village" and other outposts, and ends with "The Ritual":

"The first time on record, the rhythms and musical sounds of secret and highest orders of native tribes are used to transform the jungle mat into a colorful stage for the violent emotional expressions of these mysterious and primitive folk."

Baxter never profited off the Exotica craze to the extent that Denny and Lyman did, but he was nonetheless a guiding force.

His "Quiet Village" would become one of the most covered Exotica tunes recorded.

Baxter's early inclination to experiment with the intermittent use of a foreign instrument or two pegged him as a musical pioneer. For listeners of classic pops and standard instrumentals, this was savage stuff.

As early as 1950 Baxter's exotic music inspired classically trained composers, arrangers, and musicians to "import."

Legend of Yma

Though she was not inclined to walk around with gold coins strapped to her forehead, Yma Sumac's life faintly resembled the exotic princess depicted on her album covers.

Taboo Vol. 2
New Exotic Sounds of Arthur Lyman
HiFi Records, 1958
Photographed in Brazil

Sumac was born in a Peruvian town high in the Andes and was discovered while performing in a local festival. She was married at fourteen and a star across South America before she was twenty, using Incan and other folk songs as vehicles for her remarkable voice.

A zesty, if dubious, biographical footnote held Sumac to be descended from Inca royalty. Skeptics insisted she was just Amy Camus, a Jewish

Voice of the Xtabay
Yma Sumac
Capitol Records, 1950
Photo: Tom Kelley

housewife from Brooklyn who simply reversed her name. No evidence exists to support this claim.

In the late 1940s, Sumac and her then-husband, Moises Vivanco, came to the United States, achieving minor renown in New York nightclubs and the "Borscht Belt" resorts of the Catskills. A Capitol Records scout "discovered" Sumac in a nightclub, and in 1950, the label released, and Baxter produced, *Voice of the Xtabay*, her rendition of Peruvian folk songs. The cover depicts Sumac as a sorceress crooning beneath a floating statue of a demigod while a volcano erupts in the background.

Sumac's sirenic voice sailed above hyperbole. It ranged from four to five octaves, and *Voice of the Xtabay* sold a half million copies with little advertising.

For her 1957 album, *Legend of the Jivaro*, Sumac and Vivanco traveled to the Amazon to live with headhunters, according to the liner notes.

Jungle fever quickly spread to unsuspecting studio musicians and arrangers.

On *Voodoo!*, musician and arranger Richard Haymen bravely takes listeners on a musical adventure into the deepest interior of Haiti: "This is music to be met halfway in a quiet room with the lights dimmed. Or better still meet it all the way in the still of the night with the lights out. Then listen!

"You're not alone any longer. The room is shaken with the frantic dances of the hungans—so called priests of

Legend of the Jivaro

In ancient times, the Jivaros, being neighbors of the highly cultured Incas, were comparatively civilized. However, the advent of the Spanish conquistadores in the sixteenth century greatly altered their lives. Their temples were looted, their treasures stolen, their villages destroyed. Thus it was that the Jivaros lived in their remote mountainous jungles, alone and bitter, hating the white man, reverting to near Stone-Age existence that included the practice of head-shrinking.

Sumac and her husband, Moises Vivanco, went into Jivaro country armed only with trinkets, good intentions, and a tape recorder. Fortunately the Jivaros proved friendly and Vivanco was able to tape innumerable native sounds and melodies. Using strange native Jivaro instruments and the elements of Jivaro life—stones, pots, pieces of wood, and bones, Yma and Vivanco captured Jivaro life.

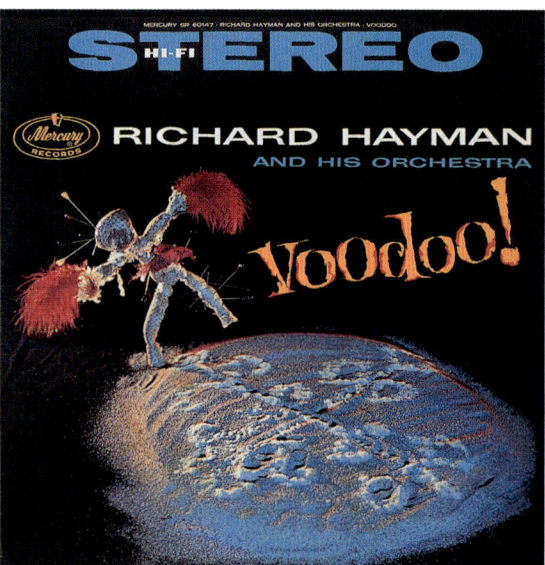

Voodoo!
Richard Haymen and His Orchestra
Mercury Records, 1959

voodoo—and their faithful. The cauldron boils and froths. The walls echo to the cries and the wails of the believers. That's voodoo."

Tiki Exotica

Throughout the 1950s Hawaii's looming statehood was a mainland fascination.

Traditional Hawaiian and Polynesian records had earned a comfortable home in the living rooms across America, just like hula dances, luaus, Tiki bars, and outdoor grilling had become a part of the national consciousness.

One night, Martin Denny was playing his usual gig at a Honolulu nightclub, when he experienced a musical revelation. While he played Baxter's "Quiet Village," some frogs began to croak in time with the music. The band improvised some birdcalls as a joke. The next night the audience was requesting more. In 1957 Denny recorded *Exotica*. In 1959 "Quiet Village"—included on the album—became a hit.

Denny mined the sounds of Africa, Europe, and the Orient to make thirty-six more albums including *Hypnotique, Primitiva, Exotica II,* and *AfroDesia*.

Shortly after *Exotica*, Denny's vibraphonist, Arthur Lyman, replaced him at the bar and took the island sound down roads of his own.

His first album, *Taboo* (1958), became a huge seller. Included on the album are sounds "from actual birds...and congas, bongos, tymbali, cocktail drums, boobams, cowbell, asses' jaw, conch shell, and quido, as well as the more ordinary percussions."

On *Taboo Vol. 2,* Lyman covers "Ebb Tide," "Moon of Manakoora," and Baxter's "Love Dance." "The disc places you in the midst of the pulsating, brooding, yet heart-quickening African Jungle. You close your eyes and listen to the birdcalls, the strange sounds in the jungle night."

Reportedly the shrunken heads on the cover were photographed in the "savage jungles" of Brazil.

By the late 1950s there were hundreds of Hawaiian records—from traditional to the truly bizarre.

Hawaii cast a gentle spell on Brooklyn-bred Leo Addeo—RCA arranger and the label's unofficial Hawaiian music specialist. On *Hawaiian Paradise,* Addeo combined instrumentals with island-style choral arrangements. The liner notes claim "you can almost hear the soft wind rustling the palm trees and the warm Pacific gliding up and down the glistening beaches." Pay no mind to the fact that the music was recorded in a New York studio.

Addeo believed *Hawaii in Hi-Fi* was a step ahead, noting "a fullness of clarity, not innocent of echo chambers, that will intrigue even those dedicated owners of hi-fi units who up until now have given Hawaii little thought except to wonder how long before it would be the fiftieth state."

Pianist Ernie Warren's *A Latin from Manhattan in Hawaii* illustrates either America's proud history of multiculturalism or the industry's co-optation of new trends.

The album includes imperialist favorites such as "Little Brown Gal" and "Pretty Maui Girl" along with provocative Latin rhythms from countries, as the liner notes suggests, "natively tempestuous and restless, and like the people that inhabit them, the music has a very tangible excitement."

Taboo
The Cwanda Group
Promenade Records
late 1950s

The Sounds of Exotic
Island
The Surfmen
*Somerset Records,
late 1950s*
Photo: George Pickow
Cover art: Will Dressler

Bahia
*The Exotic Sounds of
Arthur Lyman*
HiFi Records, 1959

Noteworthy Jungle and Tiki Films

Cannibal Women in the Avocado Jungle of Death
Dr. Cyclops
Tarzan, the Ape Man
Troma's War
White Pongo
Mondo Cane
Island of Lost Souls
Mysterious Island
Pagan Island
Paradise, Hawaiian Style
Taboo   **South Pacific**

Tropical Cruise
*Pedro Garcia and His
Del Prado Orchestra
Audio Fidelity, 1957
Photo: Bob Witt*

A Tropical Affair
*Pedro Garcia and His
Del Prado Orchestra
Audio Fidelity, 1957
Photo: Bob Witt*

Jungle and Tiki Songs

In the 1950s and 1960s the Polynesian God Tiki was resurrected by tourists to the islands. In their return suitcases were crudely carved Tiki statuettes.

Back home, with Tiki watching from the mantle, they danced to these Polynesian rhythms:

"Hawaiian War Chant"
Music by Johnny Noble and Leileohaka from traditional Hawaiian chant, "Tahu Wahu Wahi."
English lyrics by Ralph Freed
Tommy Dorsey made the tune swing in 1939.

"Hawaiian Wedding Song"
Words by Al Hoffman, Dick Manning
Music, Hawaiian words by Charles E. King
Andy Williams had a huge hit with the song in 1958.

"Moon of Manakoora"
Words by Frank Loesser
Music by Alfred Newman
The theme song for the 1930s ecological adventure film *The Hurricane*, starring Dorothy Lamour. Manakoora was the tropical island on which the film took place.

"Quiet Village"
Written by Les Baxter for his second album, *Ritual of the Savage*, in 1952, Martin Denny took the song to the top of the charts in 1959.

Island Instruments

Bamboo
Used as a wind instrument all over Polynesia.

Hawaiian guitar
A steel guitar laid across the knees for the left hand to make the notes by pressing the strings with a bar held straight across them.

Kettledrum
A heavy upright drum carved from a tree trunk.

Pahu
A drum carved from palm wood with a head of sharkskin. Played with fingers and hand.

Ukulele
The small four-stringed guitar was introduced to the Hawaiian Islands by the Portuguese in the nineteenth century. *Ukulele* literally means "little flea." The name is believed to have been the nickname of an officer who was a keen performer on it.

Xylophone
A percussion instrument of tuned wooden bars. Common in parts of Africa, Central America, Asia, and the Western world. Similar to the marimba and vibraphone.

The 50th State
Charles Bud Dant and His Orchestra
*Coral Records,
late 1950s*

Lure of the Islands
Hal Aloma and the Hawaiian Orchestra
Dot Records, late 1950s
Photo courtesy of United Airlines

Lotus Land
Gene Rains
Decca Records, late 1950s

Dance the Hula in the Moonlight
Danny Stewart and His Orchestra
*Coral Records,
late 1950s*
Model: Mealii Horio of the Hawaiian Room at the Hotel Lexington

Hawaii in Hi-Fi
Leo Addeo and His Orchestra
RCA Camden, 1959

Latin Fire
Westinghouse
promotional record
Columbia Records,
early 1960s

The Latin Invasion

In the 1950s North America was unhinged by a fiery Latin dance called the mambo, the biggest and wildest dance craze the continent had ever seen.

Cuban bandleader Xavier Cugat had already introduced some of the motions of South America in the 1930s and 1940s with the rumba, samba, conga, and a revival of the 1920s tango.

Entrepreneurial dance instructor Arthur Murray assumed the responsibility of teaching these exciting new dances.

Through Murray's records, an accompanying TV show, and dance school franchises, you could "ballroom" dance without living in Miami or New York or belonging to a country club.

The frenzy began in earnest in the early 1950s with Perez Prado's first major record, *Mambo Jambo*.

His swingin'-jazz style was invigorating. The five-foot-six Prado blew everyone away with four saxes, four trumpets, one trombone, bass drum, snare drum, congas, and bongos.

Mambo Jambo
Perez Prado
RCA Victor,
early 1950s
Cover art: Charles Meggs
Photo: Ron Vogel

He became known for his grunts. The liner notes to *Mambo Jambo* explained: "One word that Prado does know…one that has no generic root is 'ugh!' Perez also uses a number of Spanish and Mexican words to his compatriots and to his band…the most common, 'dilo,' which freely translated would mean 'say it,' but when used by Señor Prado it changes abruptly to something roughly resembling the English phrase 'make it happen,' and this is the one word…'dilo' that he barks at the section and the soloists of his band."

In 1958 RCA released *Dilo Ugh!*

Tito Puente, a four-time Grammy winner and one of the U.S.'s most popular Latin jazz musicians, contributed to the mambo craze and Latin music in general with more than one hundred albums and performances. He delivered feverish arrangements with *Mamborama* and *Mambo with Me*.

Longtime rival and Puerto Rican bandleader-arranger Tito Rodriguez was the third mambo king.

During the 1940s Rodriguez played briefly with Cugat and then Noro Morales. He then formed a band called the Mambo Devils, which he soon disbanded. In the 1950s he recorded several albums with Tico Records that were especially popular with Latin audiences.

For the mambo he recorded *Mambo Madness*. Madness indeed:

- In 1954 Perry Como sang "Papa Loves to Mambo," and Rosemary Clooney topped the charts with "Mambo Italiano."
- Peruvian diva Yma Sumac lured large groups of people from their daily responsibilities with songs like "Chicken Talk," and "Five Bottles Mambo" from her album *Mambo!*

Prado, Puente, Cugat, and Rodriguez were

vintage mambo (in American terms), but there were countless knockoff dance records to choose from. Bongos and a mambo beat could spice up practically any tune.

Soon, the mambo had to clear the floor for a milder, simpler dance: the cha-cha.

Puente released *Cha Cha Cha for Lovers, Dance the Cha Cha Cha, Let's Cha Cha with Puente,* and *Mucho Cha-Cha.*

Rodriguez countered Puente's cha-cha with his *Motion Picture Themes Cha Cha Cha.*

It seemed that for some the only requirement of a cha-cha tune was that the music be faster and a "cha cha cha" be added at the end: On *B'Way Cha Chas* Fred Sateriale and His Big Band play "Old Man River ChaChaCha" and "Smoke Gets in Your Eyes, ChaChaCha."

Whenever it seemed a dance was getting old, the kings would pull a forgotten one out of oblivion or create a new one of their own.

Prado invented the bongoson—a marriage of the twist and the Cuban dance, the son. Rodriguez presented the Wa-Pa-Cha—the cha-cha with hand clapping. But it was not enough. By the late 1950s the Latin dance craze dwindled, replaced by the twists and turns of American teens.

In 1961 Perez Prado invented "Rockambo" to describe "today's red hot music, overlaid with a swinging Latin-American beat." A year later he tried again to renew interest in Latin music with *The Twists Goes Latin.* But the resuscitation failed. Rock and roll would not budge.

Beyond Dance

The various dance crazes spurred interest in Latin music in general. Consequently, record companies churned out "authentic" recordings from all over Latin America.

Many American easy-listening artists were seduced by Latin sounds. To announce their conversion, some named albums after themselves, simply adding a suffix like "Goes Latin."

The Latin musicians, or their American impersonators, authenticated their recordings by making a song "sound" indigenous or, as often was the case with American artists, arranging a quintessential Latin tune with a full orchestra.

- On the 1960 record *The Sacred Idol,* Les Baxter combines his trademark orchestral effects with primitive rhythms to portray the Spanish conquistadors' sixteenth century invasion of the land of the Aztecs.
- On *Carnival Tropical,* "classics for the masses" conductor André Kostelanetz leads his orchestra in selections by Latin American composers, such as

Maria Elena
Los Indios Tabajaras
RCA Victor, 1963

Ernesto Lecuona, whose songs were covered frequently by Space Age Pop musicians and arrangers.

In a similar vein, American favorites often got a Latin "twist."

Los Indios Tabajaras on *The Mellow Guitar Moods of Los Indios Tabajaras* (1963), throw a new light on American perennials "St. Louis Blues" and "Sunrise Serenade" with their "lilting tropical sway…For once we hear these songs as they sound to the ears of the South American Indian."

Los Indios Tabajaras were billed as two Brazilian Indians who chanced upon a guitar left by white men in the middle of the jungle. The young boys taught themselves to play the instrument. They loved it enough to want to follow it into the white man's world from where it had come. The story maintains that they were discovered by an agent while playing a gig in Rio de Janeiro.

After touring South America for several years, they decided to study the classics. Soon they were playing Bach, Beethoven, and Chopin and touring Europe, where they learned to sing and speak in Italian, German, and Greek, in addition to their native Tupi, Portuguese, and Spanish.

From 1943 through the 1960s they recorded several albums for RCA, mainly for the South American market.

On *Maria Elena*, the duo played a simple version of "Maria Elena," a thirty year-old Mexican tune, on acoustic guitars and without a single change of key. Its success was 1963's strangest hit-parade story. *Maria Elena* reached sales of 250,000 in Britain and more than 500,000 in Italy. The record industry was astounded.

It seemed the entire world had surrendered to the Latin Invasion.

The Dances of the People

In contrast to the smooth, sophisticated movement of classic dances such as the tango and fox trot, Latin and Caribbean dances are up-tempo, primal, hot, and marked by a strong simple rhythm.

These dances often were performed at festivals and carnivals.

The rhythm finds expression in the dancer's body through a relaxing and straightening of the knees and a movement of the hips.

Cha-Cha
Basically a mambo rhythm played in a slower tempo. Where the mambo is unrestrained and aggressive, the cha-cha is more subtle and soft.

Mambo
The mambo is a fusion of Afro-Cuban rhythms with a big-band format adopted from swing jazz. The mambo is the fastest of the Cuban dances.

Rumba
The erotic, sensual dance combines African and Cuban rhythms. The dance reached the U.S. in the 1920s.

Samba
A Brazilian-style dance with African origins. Before World War II Carmen Miranda, the "Brazilian bombshell," created a samba rage in America.

Lecuona's Music In Dance Tempos
Orquesta Havana Casino
K Ubaney, late 1950s

Ernesto Lecuona

Ernesto Lecuona's songs have been recorded hundreds of times by jazz, easy listening, and Exotica artists.

Also a pianist and bandleader, Lecuona is probably one of the most successful composers Cuba has produced. His niece, Margarita, also helped write some songs, most notably "Tabu" and "Babalu."

Most Exotica and Space Age Pop artists have recorded one, if not all, of the following Lecuona songs:

"The Breeze and I"

"The Peanut Vendor"

"Malaguena"

"Jungle Drums"

"Siboney"

"Taboo (Tabu)"

"Babalu"

Cha Cha Cha's for Lovers
Tito Puente
Tico Records, late 1950s
Cover art: Lee–Myles Associates

Faz
Roberto Faz and His Group
Puchito Records
Photo: Mary and Renny, folkloric dancers

In addition to Hugo Winterhalter's **Winterhalter Goes...Latin,** Mantovani had a **Latin Rendezvous;** George Shearing, **A Latin Escapade;** Henry Mancini, **Mr. Lucky Goes Latin;** Martin Denny, **Spanish Village;** Richard Haymen, **Genuine Electric Latin Love Machine;** Percy Faith, **Malaguena;** and Lenny Dee, **Dee-Latin**

Carnival Tropicana
André Kostelanetz and His Orchestra
Columbia Records, late 1950s

Latin American Stylings
José Melis
Mercury Records, 1957

Manhattan Latin
Dave Pike
*Decca Records,
late 1950s*

Continental Tangos
Marcel Feijoo
Decca Records, 1957

Cha Cha Cha for Swingin' Partners
Pupi Prado and Orchestra
Celebrity Records, late 1950s

Rumba on a Cloud
Los Rumberos De Cuba
Tico Recording Company, late 1950s

Mambo in Havana
Unattributed
Riveria Records, mid-1950s

Orienta
The Markko Polo Adventurers
RCA Victor, 1959

The Exotic East

A whiff of jasmine, a flash of jade.
A winding street in Singapore.
A sheik's caravan, laden with precious baubles.
An island outrigger on a moon-drenched beach.
A multicolored bird in a jungle glade.
A tropical breeze, like sandalwood and wine.
Mystery peering through beaded curtains.

—From Axel Stordahl's Jasmine and Jade, 1959

As some artists mined the music and culture of Polynesia and Latin America, others "traveled" from India to Bulgaria in search of the exotic fruits of the East. The record labels also "discovered" talent, and a few genuine articles in search of fame found their way across the seas.

Sondi
Sondi Sodsai
Liberty Records, 1958
Photo: Garrett-Howard

Axel Stordahl notes on his Eastern-inspired *Jasmine and Jade* that he evokes the enchanted land "without the use of animal noises and birdcalls."

With the standard Exotica repertoire of songs—"Baubles, Bangles and Beads," "The Moon of Manakoora," "Caravan," and "Bali Ha'i," Stordahl "took great pains to create his effects using only actual musical instruments."

Many artists juxtaposed East and West to highlight the musical and cultural differences, not to mention a few stereotypes.

• In 1960 Japanese-American Tak Shindo recorded those differences on *Brass and Bamboo*. Shindo blends a standard big-band arrangement of the West—brass, flutes, clarinets, drums, and bass—with exotic instruments of Japan—the koto, Kabuki drums, samisen, bamboo flutes, gongs, and an assortment of bells and chimes.

• On the 1959 album *Orienta*, the Markko Polo Adventurers combine the charm of the Orient with the "wit of the Occident."

Or as the liner notes state: "It resembles the dreams of an imaginative person who has fallen asleep during a 'Dr. Fu Manchu' movie on television."

Beginning with "Yokahama Ferryboat" and ending with "Runaway Rickshaw," a song depicting a boy pulling an overweight tourist uphill, the Adventurers use sound effects to tell stories of humor, romance, intrigue, and life across the Orient.

In addition to Pat Suzuki, star of *The Flower Drum Song*, there were many "young women" from the East vying for a spot in America's heart.

• On *Sondi* (1958), Sondi Sodsai, "the Girl with the Happy Face" interprets American hits like "Love Is a Many Splendored Thing" and "Bali Ha'i." "And if you are listening to this record in stereo," the liner notes claim, "you will actually see Sondi dancing across the floor in front of you."

Now that's stereo!

Sodsai, a UCLA student at the time of the recording, grew up in Thailand where reportedly she was an entertainer to the royal court.

- Kapp Records promoted an Armenian-American, Anita Darian, as the next Yma Sumac, making the bold claim that Darian had a greater vocal range than Sumac. Unfortunately, the two never had a screaming match.

In the 1950s and 1960s Darian toured with the Sauter-Finegan Orchestra, and appeared in opera houses, hotels, and supper clubs. On *East of the Sun,* she renders Armenian folk songs such as "Hoy Nar" and "Anoush Karoon."

- Years before Indian composer and musician Ravi Shankar inspired the sitar fad in rock, turban-wearing Korla Pandit entranced listeners with his hypnotic organ playing.

Avowing that his personal goal was much the same as Gandhi's, Pandit sought to bring love and understanding to all people through the "universal language of music."

Like Lenny Dee, Pandit was able to produce from the organ the sounds of violins, flutes, brass, bells, and drums. In 1949 he appeared in one of the first all-musical TV program in Hollywood. In the 1950s he starred in a one-hour weekly show.

Pandit recorded fourteen records with Fantasy. He continued to play through the 1960s and 1970s, touring mainly on the West Coast.

Other Exotica artists hopped on the caravan to India. Martin Denny "traveled halfway around the world to India. He returned with the authentic sounds of the sitar, tabla, and tamboura," all of which he used in *A Taste of India.* The album features Western music "flavored with the mystical embellishments of Eastern musical culture."

The Gypsy in My Soul

There would be no culture left untouched. Space Age Pop artists toured all of Europe looking for real gypsy music, producing album covers that usually featured a smoldering dark-haired, dark-eyed gypsy woman dancing vigorously.

After *Hugo Winterhalter Goes...Latin,* there was *Winterhalter Goes...Gypsy.* On *Gypsy,* he captures the contrasting moods of gypsy music—from sultry themes to fiery, spirited numbers with songs like "Golden Earrings" and "Gypsy Love Song."

André Kostelanetz even boasted a "genuine" gypsy fiddler on *Gypsy Passion.*

East of the Sun
Anita Darian
Kapp Records,
late 1950s

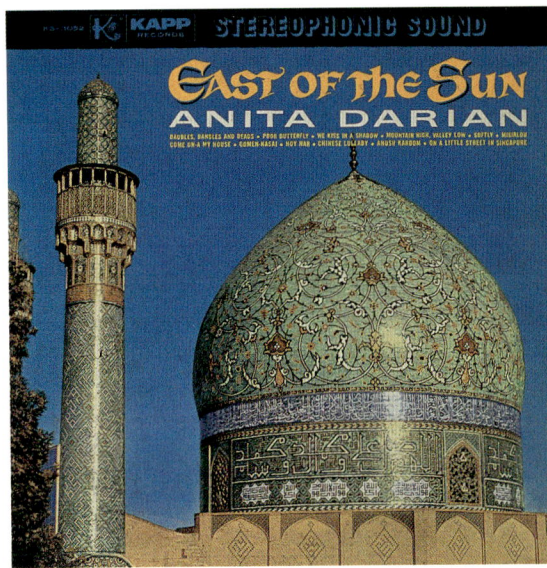

Jasmine and Jade
Axel Stordahl
Dot Records, 1959
Photo: Max Yavno

Eastern Instruments

Boo Bams (*bamboo* turned around) Tuned sections of bamboo with skins that act as percussion heads.

Burmese gongs Sonorous gongs used in Buddhist temples during ceremonial rites.

Celestette A miniature celeste.

Koto (or Japanese Long Zither) One of Japan's great classical stringed instruments.

Piccolo xylophone A small, high-pitched xylophone.

Samisen A Japanese lute with three strings.

Temple blocks Hollow wooden percussion instrument made of camphor wood carved into a skull-like shape with a wide slit-like mouth. Originally used in Confucian ceremonies.

Wind chimes Small pieces of glass that have been used by the Japanese to ward off evil spirits. They produce a beautiful tinkling sound.

Wood chimes Bamboo of different lengths, sealed at each end and strung together with twine. A delicate, woody sound.

Port Said
Music of the Middle East
Mohammed El-Bakkar
and His Oriental Ensemble
Audio Fidelity, 1958
Cover model: Nejla Ates

How to Make Your Husband a Sultan

I Remember Lebanon and *Port Said* are examples of belly dancing records popular in the 1950s.

By creating an oversexualized Middle East, the music inspired a dress rehearsal for the sexual revolution of the next decade. Because it was presented as "belly dancing music," an import from another culture, society accepted it.

Housewives learned to belly dance for their elated husbands. The upbeat, wild music tried to evoke images of exotic slave girls, as does this passage from the liner notes to *Oriental Fantasy*:

"I am sure that the Persian Market musically described here sold all sorts of flying carpets, magic lamps whose genii performed all sorts of useful tasks, to say nothing of lovely Circassian slave girls who also performed tasks that were a little more believable."

With drums, flutes, bells, cymbals, castanets, clarinets, oboes, strings, and percussion sticks, tenor Mohammed El-Bakkar presents on *Port Said* a native setting harking back to "the ancient slave market, when maidens performed sensuous and provocative dances to the accompanient [sic] of native bands of musicians."

The cover of *Port Said* (1958), features Nejla Ates, a dancer at the time in the Broadway musical *Fanny*, about a French girl who, assuming her lover to be lost at sea, marries an older man.

I Remember Lebanon
*Wadih-El-Safi and Najah Salam
Fiesta Records,
late 1950s
Photo: Three Lions Studio
Cover design:
Victor Mikus*

The *Esquire* Album of Music for the Continental Host
Guy Lupar and His Orchestra
Esquire and RCA Victor, 1956

Music for Sipping Martinis

*W*hat red-blooded American male beyond the age of innocence does not want to act the Continental host?

—The *Esquire* Album of Music for the Continental Host

Cocktail music can be swingin', sultry, jazzy, Latin-infused, even exotic, but it must keep the drinks coming. From the 1950s into the 1960s, lounge acts, piano trios, chanteuses, and good, stiff cocktail records provided hours of entertainment for sipping sophisticates.

The Lounge Act, Vegas Style

During its heyday in the mid-1950s, the lounge scene was dominated by such performers and Vegas standards as George Raft, Jimmy Durante, and Louis Prima. Their goal was to make listeners have fun and keep buying drinks.

At the Sahara Casino's famed Casbah Lounge, Prima, wife Keely Smith, sax player Sam

Butera, and the Witnesses entertained wildly into the early morning hours.

With a clowning manner and wacky songs like "Pleeza No Squeeza da Banana" and "Just a Gigolo/I Ain't Got Nobody," Prima delivered riotous performances against Smith's subdued and deadpan presence.

Word-of-mouth popularity started packing the club in the early 1950s. Capitol Records took notice. By 1957 Prima had recorded *The Wildest*, *Call of the Wildest*, and *The Wildest Show at Tahoe*.

The Cocktail Pianist

The cocktail pianist provided the perfect accompaniment to hors d'oeuvres, drinks, and an occasional spin on the dance floor.

His duty was less to entertain than to set an atmosphere conducive to chatter, clatter, and countless toasts.

Irving Fields was the classic cocktail pianist. Fields and his trio played such velvet-lined and smoky New York lounges as the Emerald Room and Mermaid Room. Devotees gathered to drink and smoke and listen to "Managua Nicaragua," "Persian Pearl," and "Miami Beach Rumba."

• Denny and Lyman had their own brand of cocktail—exotic—which conformed to cocktail sipping amid pagan gods, tiki huts, and palm trees.

• Jazz pianist George Shearing, on the other hand, was straight up. No animal cries, just smooth and subtle, baby.

• Lenny Dee and Don Baker stretched the limits of the cocktail pianist.

With their help, the churchly Hammond organ was soon off the wagon and into the lounge.

Baker and his trio made their home on the Vegas Strip; Dee settled south at the Plantation Club in Nashville, and later at Lenny Dee's Den on the beach in St. Petersburg, Florida.

Dee injected a since unmatched moodiness and vitality into the priggish Hammond.

The Chanteuse

With streamlined glamour, raw sex appeal, and sequined gowns, lounge sirens such as Abbe Lane and Julie London could drive many a lonely guy to drink. There was little innuendo. The songs were straight up. Take London's "The Man That Got Away": "A jigger of lying/garnished with fights/some bitters for crying/long unhappy nights/a dash of lost dreams/then stir with regret/shake well and pour/then drink and forget."

London first performed live in 1955 at Los Angeles' intimate 881 Club. Torch singers passionately belted out numbers—London delivered chilling, intoxicating melodies.

In 1955 she signed with Liberty Records. Her first album, *Julie Is Her Name*, included her biggest hit, "Cry Me a River."

Liquor-Infused Living Rooms

In the 1950s and into the Kennedy years, cocktail parties at home became an after-work norm for middle-class Americans, making cocktail records the necessary accompaniment.

Record labels provided on vinyl all the great live acts, as well as cocktail collections.

In addition to Prima, London, and all the best, there was *Music for Playboys to Play By*, *Be There at Five*, and *Cocktails for Two*.

The Great One

Jackie Gleason tapped into America's love for the cocktail and in-home entertainment with a series of successful Capitol recordings.

Gleason had already earned a place in American households as a comedian and star of the 1950s TV show *The Honeymooners*, and this popularity fueled the release of more than twenty albums for Capitol between 1952 and 1969. Musically illiterate, Gleason created his albums by simply describing the sounds he imagined to the studio musicians and arrangers.

William A. Henry III, in *The Great One: The Life and Legend of Jackie Gleason*, notes that Gleason commonly favored rather crude analogies.

Jackie Gleason presents "Oooo!"
Jackie Gleason with the Voices of Artie Malvin
Capitol Records, 1957

Outside the lounge, London lent her provocative presence to such films as *The Voice in the Mirror*, *The Great Man*, and *The George Raft Story*.

Julie London
Julie London
Guest Star Records,
early 1960s

Once he instructed the orchestra to make "the sound of pissing off a high bridge into a teacup."

Despite the ad hoc nature of the production, his first LP, *Music for Lovers Only* (1952), sold 500,000 copies.

Songs from the album, such as "My Funny Valentine" and "I'm in the Mood for Love" conjured "a wisp of cigarette smoke in the soft lamplight, the tinkle of a glass, a hushed whisper...and music for lovers only." In 1953 Gleason followed with the lovesick *Lover's Rhapsody*, which had "muted strings and softly singing reeds."

Music, Martinis and Memories (1954) was the perfect companion for cocktail parties. *Lover's Portfolio* (1961) included drink recipes. Many of the albums featured former Glenn Miller trumpeter Bobby Hackett and guitarists Tony Mottola and Al Caiola.

While Gleason realized his music was, as he once put it, "plain vanilla," he understood the appeal of a good album cover.

"Gleason's records catered blatantly to the common man's lusts," says Joseph Lanza in *Elevator Music*. "Silk-and-lace-dishabilled vixens reclining on sofas; hopeful sirens leering with come-hither lips; jeweled femmes fatale straddling bar stools; and Nordic nymphs lurking in dark forests. This was mood music for men who may not have been up on the latest Kinsey findings but appreciated a good trollop on the pages of *Cavalier*."

Gleason provided musical accompaniment to nights alone and cocktail parties. The Three Suns, in comparison, sought to spice things up a bit. The Suns' unique and unexpected treatment of songs were required listening after a few drinks.

Reportedly Mamie Eisenhower's favorite band, The Suns had a hit in 1944 with "Twilight Time," and another in 1947 with their cover of the Harmonicats' "Peg o' My Heart."

On the 1961 *Fever & Smoke*, the trio plays a marimba, vibraphone, Salvation Army drum, kettledrum, and a Fender bass, and they were the first trio to use a guitar-organ-accordion combination.

Despite their musical originality, their album covers used the conventional theme of the era—the solitary woman in heat.

Cocktail covers feature a wide range of solicitous women. Collectors now refer to these as "Cheesecake" or "Sleazecake," and collect them for the covers alone. Chanteuse Abbe Lane adorns a few, as does Julie London, whose album *Calender Girl* features a Julie for every month. Smitten male listeners undoubtedly were pleasantly surprised when they opened the inside fold to find an extra-large picture of Julie for the "thirteenth" month.

The Best of Xavier Cugat
Xavier Cugat
*Mercury Records,
late 1950s*
Model: Abbe Lane

Champagne Dancing Party
Lawrence Welk
Coral Records, 1960

Other great cocktail records include:
On the Rocks
Bob Thompson
The Eyes of Love
Hugo Winterhalter
I'm Glad There's You
Vic Damone
Mr. Piano
Roger Williams

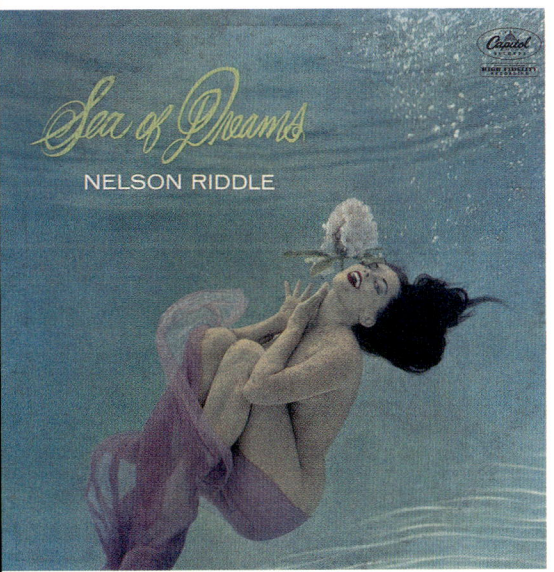

Sea of Dreams
Nelson Riddle
Capitol Records, 1957
Photo: Tom Kelley

Music for Playboys to Play By
Hollywood Playboys Orchestra
Urania Records, late 1950s

Businessman's Bounce:
Music for the Expense Account Set
Eddie LeMar
Warner Bros. Records, 1958
Photo: Hal Adams

Fever & Smoke
The Three Suns
RCA Victor, 1961

Mr. Piano
Roger Williams
Kapp Records,
early 1960s

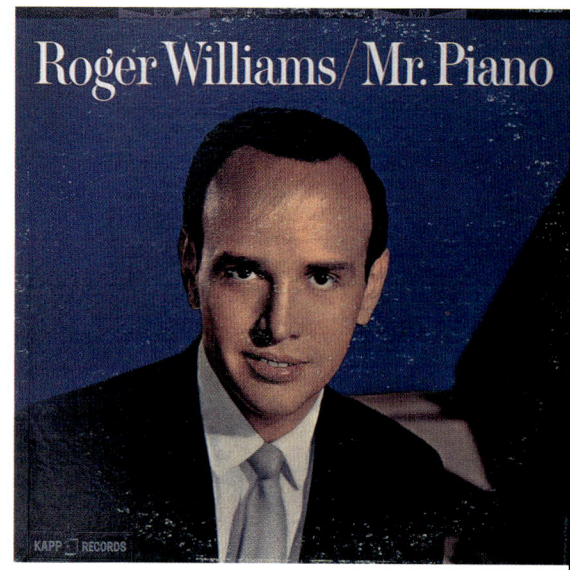

Be There at 5:
Conversational Music for
Cocktails
Compilation
Mercury Records, 1957

For cocktails, keep in mind:
Mose Allison
Count Basie
Xavier Cugat
Vic Damone
Sammy Davis Jr.
Eydie Gorme
Steve Lawrence
Dean Martin
Frank Sinatra
Mel Torme
Dionne Warwick

Cocktail Time
The Three Suns
Rondo-Lette Records,
early 1950s

From Another World
Sid Bass
Vik Records, 1956
Photo: Wendy Hilty

The Sounds of Space

The technology born of America's space yen had an enormous impact on its citizens' daily lives. Signs of space were seen in home furnishings, appliances, cars, and, of course, entertainment equipment.

Science fiction films, such as *Invaders from Mars*, presented space as full of little green aliens. Others took a serious approach. *Invasion of the Body Snatchers* is a frightening film about small-town residents being replaced by inert duplicates hatched from alien pods. The film's McCarthy-era subtext makes it even more scary.

Recording artists, in turn, created what they imagined space to "sound" like.

The result was silly and fun, and at times, dreamy and eerie.

Musicians, arrangers, and electronic-music pioneers used America's fascination with space (and theirs) as a vehicle for presenting out-of-this-world sounds.

For the 1956 film *Forbidden Planet*, electronic-music experimenters Louis and

Soundproof
Ferrante and Teicher
Westminster, 1956
Cover photo: M.G.M.
Pictures

The Theremin

The theremin was invented in the 1920s by Russian physicist Leon Theremin. The instrument is played by the motions of the hands in the air over an electronic field. The right hand gives pitch, the left volume.

- *Les Baxter used it on his 1951 album Music out of the Moon.*
- *The Day the Earth Stood Still featured two theremins.*
- *One of the greatest theremenists was Clara Rockmore, whose record features her playing Tchaikovsky and Rachmaninoff.*

Bebe Barron manipulated tape and electronic instruments, such as the theremin, to create the first fully electronic soundtrack.

They used cybernetic circuits to create sounds expressing a particular feeling for each scene. They then processed the resulting sounds by altering the pitch or speed. The Barrons didn't even consider it music, but it was nominated for an Academy Award nonetheless.

After the film, the theremin became synonymous with space music and added a super-eerie feel to films such as Alfred Hitchcock's *Spellbound*.

Another milestone in electronic instrumentation also occurred in the mid-1950s, when RCA unveiled the first instrument that wasn't played at all—the synthesizer.

The synthesizer "played itself" by way of a "synthesist" who punched codes into a roll of paper. The equipment then compiled the song and played it back.

The label released a demonstration record of the synthesizer simulating musical instruments and a human voice. While hardly practical for the studio, it foretold the future.

At the same time, the tape recorder added a new dimension to music. With tape, any sounds, whether acoustic or electronic, could be manipulated. During the early 1950s multitrack electric guitar stars Les Paul and Mary Ford had huge hits with such effects. Their first, "How High the Moon," sold 1.5 million copies.

Columbia Records showcased tape effects on *Delirium in Hi-Fi* (1956), by Elsa Popping and Her Pixieland Band (composer André Popp). The album included tape reversal, phase shifting, and speed manipulation.

America was widely introduced to electronic music through radio and television commercials, many of which were arranged by pioneers Raymond Scott and Eric Siday.

- On their space-inspired album *Soundproof* (1956), piano duo Arthur Ferrante and Louis Teicher used seventeen channels and seventeen microphones on movable suspended booms to achieve "the last word in effects recording."

On another Ferrante and Teicher space album, *Blast Off!,* the two play their modified pianos (with bits of wood, metal bars, and other gadgets stuck in the stringbed) to songs like "I Got Rhythm" and "Chopstick Cha Cha."

These albums were made during the duo's experimental days of the 1950s—when they were creating "electronic" noises—before they became purveyors of sentimental easy-listening.

- The master of unusual arrangements, Esquivel, uses no gimmicks on *Other Worlds Other Sounds*. He does use "the most super-stereophonic equipment" and a twenty-six-piece orchestra.
- On *Strings for a Space Age* (1962), Bobby Christian attempts to "radiate some of the same energy an artificial satellite generates as it is projected into space."

Like Esquivel, Christian believed that no matter how good a tune was, a new arrangement and some improvisation could make it more appealing. Side two of the album features "The Call, Preparation"; "Count-Down, Flight into Orbit & Empyrean"; "Re-Entry"; and "Finale."

"By the time the music dies away, the listener has a very clear impression of having heard through sound a trajectory which parallels that described by a missile orbited into space and pulled back to earth."

- On the 1956 space album *From Another World,* Sid Bass uses reverberations and an "unusual" combination of trombones and baritone saxophone to make such standards as "Old Devil Moon," "Stormy Weather," "My Blue Heaven," and "East of the Sun" sound galactic.
- On yet another 1950s space record, *Music from Outer Space,* dance-bandleader and film arranger Frank Comstock renders the music of "whirling satellites, brilliant galaxies, streaming comets, mysterious planets, and the eerie reaches of space in between."

In addition to his standard orchestra, Comstock used the electronic violin and theremin to add space appeal.

The In Sound from Way Out
Perrey and Kingsley
Vanguard Records, 1966

The Moog

In the 1960s pop music was changed forever with the worldwide availability of the Moog synthesizer, developed by Robert Moog. The small, keyboard-based unit could play electronic music "live."

Martin Denny was "switched on," as well as Richard Haymen (*Genuine Electric Latin Love Machine*), Sid Bass (*Moog España*), Les Baxter (*Moog Rock*), and Enoch Light (*Spaced Out*).

Before the instrument was widely available, Jean Jacques Perrey and Gershon Kingsley featured it on their albums. The result was a bizarre combination of avant garde compositions and instrumental pop.

In 1966 the duo introduced their electronic mischief to mass audiences with *The In Sound from Way Out*. The liner notes pitched it as music for the future: "Here is the electronic 'Au Go Go' that might be heard soon from the juke boxes at the interplanetary way stations where spaceships make their rest stops."

Their second album, *Kaleidoscopic Vibrations* (1967), features the ondioline and the Moog. "Baroque Hoedown" was used for years in Disneyland's Main Street electric parade.

Perrey's own *The Amazing New Electronic Pop Sound of Jean Jacques Perrey* has the Ondes Martenot, ondioline, and the Moog.

With "Island in Space," "The Little Girl from Mars," and "The Minuet of the Robots," Perrey sought to show that "there was nothing essentially 'esoteric,' or requiring a special listening apparatus, about electronic sounds and instruments."

Strings for a Space Age
Bobby Christian
Audio Fidelity, 1962

Seminal Space Films

Forbidden Planet
Based on Shakespeare's *The Tempest*, the story concerns a rescue mission to colonists on a distant planet.

Invaders from Mars
Boy cries "Martian," but nobody believes him because they have already been zapped.

Invasion of the Body Snatchers
Paranoid sci-fi epic written by Sam Peckinpah. A small California town is infiltrated by pods from outer space.

It Came from Outer Space
A man spots a spaceship crash-landing out in the desert, but can't get anyone to believe him. Music by Henry Mancini.

Plan 9 from Outer Space
Directed by Ed Wood and starring Bela Lugosi; aliens conspire to resurrect zombies and conquer Earth.

The War of the Worlds
Classic thriller about Martian invasion, based on H. G. Wells' book and Orson Welles' famous radio hoax.

The Amazing New Electronic Pop Sound of Jean Jacques Perrey
Jean Jacques Perrey
Vanguard Recording Society, 1967

The Age of Electronicus
Dick Hyman
Command Records, mid-1960s
Photos: Roger Pola/Eric Goto

Provocative Percussion, Vol. III
Enoch Light
Command Records, 1960

And Then There Was Stereo

By the time arrangers and musicians had mastered monophonic (one-channel) sound, and the record labels had agreed on a uniform system of production, stereo (two-channel) recording was developed.

The soundtrack for Walt Disney's *Fantasia*, released in the late 1930s, gave the public an idea of stereophonic music, as did the use of magnetic tape on recorders sold in the early 1950s.

The challenge to record labels became whether to promote the new stereo tape or develop stereo records.

RCA brought the idea of recording stereo on vinyl to the attention of Westrex, a subsidiary of AT&T. The label had already developed an inexpensive cutting head and compatible reproducing stylus. After a few modifications Westrex demonstrated the system in 1957.

The head of Audio Fidelity Records, Sidney Frey, was awestruck. Sensing the impend-

Dynamic Dimensions
Henri René and His
Orchestra
RCA Victor, 1961

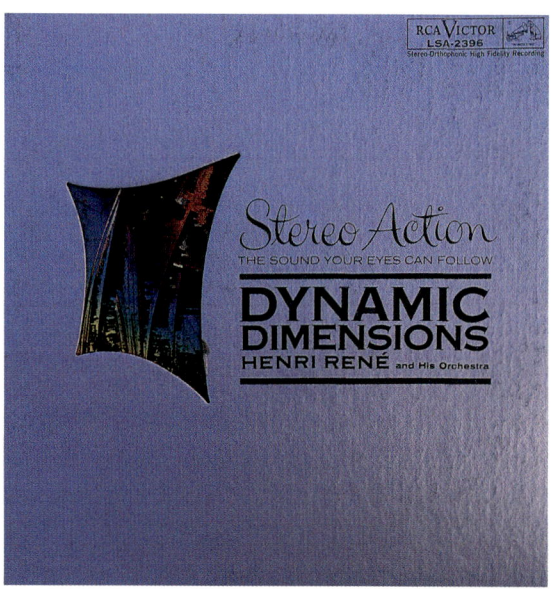

ing revolution in recorded sound, and to get publicity for his small label, he commissioned Westrex to cut a few of his LPs, including *Railroad* and *Leon Berry on the Giant Wurlitzer*.

Gimmick demonstration records, like *Railroad*, provided illusions of speeding trains, race cars, or Ping-Pong games in the living room.

The Westrex stereo production differed from that of London and Columbia. To avoid another "battle of the speeds," the Recording Industry Association of America (RIAA) adopted the Westrex system as the standard. The audio component and phonograph industry went into full stereo production. By the end of 1957 record labels cut all sessions in both monophonic and stereophonic sounds.

An even better format—the stereo tape—was available, but industry competition stalled technological Darwinism. The major tape producers, RCA and Ampex, could not agree on speeds, so consumers stuck to the records for the moment.

At its best, stereophonic recording gave music a second dimension. At its worst, original jazz and blues recordings that sounded better in monophonic were sucked up by the revolution and re-released in stereo.

By using unusual instruments from all over the world (à la Exotica), Space Age Pop musicians delivered to their listeners a double dose of unexplored sounds.

The liner notes were full of complicated charts, graphs, and audio terminology, which often took up the entire back cover, and on many records, an added inside fold.

Audiophiles found the technical data fascinating, but most trusted that the labels knew what they were talking about, and left it at that.

The record companies also tried to ensure buyers that their monophonic records would indeed still work. But they did not shy away from actively promoting the new technology.

Stereo-mania inspired bandleader and industry entrepreneur Enoch Light to start Command Records in 1959. Light capitalized from the stereo trend with a *Persuasive* and *Provocative Percussion* series to showcase sounds that "involved the listener in the substance of the music."

He was the first to use expensive 35-millimeter film tape for his master recordings (instead of magnetic tape) to produce LPs that were "the first to provide greater definition and wider range of sound."

And, as previously mentioned, Light also developed the gatefold (the inside opening fold of an album jacket), which allowed more room for liner notes and graphs, and for which Command was famous. Inside *Provocative Percussion* were instructions for listening to the songs. On "Blues in the Night": "At the opening there are rising crescendos by the bongos and by the brushes which provide a good test of your pickup response. If your pickup arm is not responding accurately, the crescendos by the bongos and brushes will seem to break up and shatter."

By the early 1960s the cry was no longer for hi-fidelity sound but for stereophonic. By 1961 seven million of the thirty million phonographs in U.S. homes were capable of playing stereophonic records.

• Somerset soon followed Command with *Perspectives in Percussion*. The label didn't provide a gatefold, but did have covers of silver paper that only literally outshined Command.

• RCA responded with *Living Stereo* and *Stereo Action*: "A conscious and deliberate effort to set music in motion by actually moving the sound of various instruments from one speaker to the other, and at times suspending it in the space between. It can smoothly float or excitingly sweep a solo instrument or group of instruments across the room before you."

• In 1961 London Records "broke the sound barriers" with *Phase 4*.

London artists like Edmundo Ros and Stanley Black made the inevitable transition into the label's *Phase 4* series. After years of recording Latin and dance tunes, Ros and Black began producing music that was stereo-infused.

Often the promotional campaign designed for an album actually competed with the artist. The cover of Xavier Cugat's *Cugat Plays Continental Hits*, part of Mercury's *Perfect Presence* series, devotes more space to the glory of 35-millimeter magnetic-film than to the talents of Cugat.

Between 1957 and the introduction of quadraphonic (four-channel) recordings in the 1970s, Space Age Pop artists made stereo an essential factor in choosing instruments and composing their music.

These musicians set their sights on recording

Cugat Plays Continental Hits
Xavier Cugat
Mercury Records,
early 1960s

albums that would not only Ping-Pong but ricochet, zigzag, spiral, and meander around every corner of the room.

The Percussion Challenge

Many artists believed percussion arrangements took full advantage of stereo. Often musicians would try to get as many drums on an album as they could fit in a studio.

The recording of Markko Polo and the Adventurers' *Orienta* (1959) was a landmark moment in percussion. During the making of the album: "The studio was virtually filled with percussion instruments, as many as twenty-five of them at one time. These were played by five of the nation's top percussionists, each of whom 'doubled' on several instruments. This astounding array of paraphernalia prompted one of the musicians to quip: 'Why don't they hire that Oriental god with six or eight arms?'"

It seemed as though musicians were in a percussion competition:

• On Marty Gold's *Skin Tight* the liner notes simply state: "This is a drum album." Gold played "Caravan," "Song of India," and "Hawaiian War Chant" with an Indian tabla, kettledrums, bongos, tom-toms, congas, woodblocks, cymbals, and cow bells.

• On *Felix Slatkin Conducts Fantastic Percussion!*, eleven percussionists play an astounding one hundred instruments of more than thirty-five types of percussion.

• Dick Schory and His Percussion Pops Orchestra boasted twenty musicians playing more than two hundred brass, string, woodwind, and percussion instruments.

• On *Wild Percussion and Horns a' Plenty*, Schory plays the "Lullaby of Broadway" and "The Peanut Vendor." The album also features "a live tap dancer…and a phony musical traffic jam."

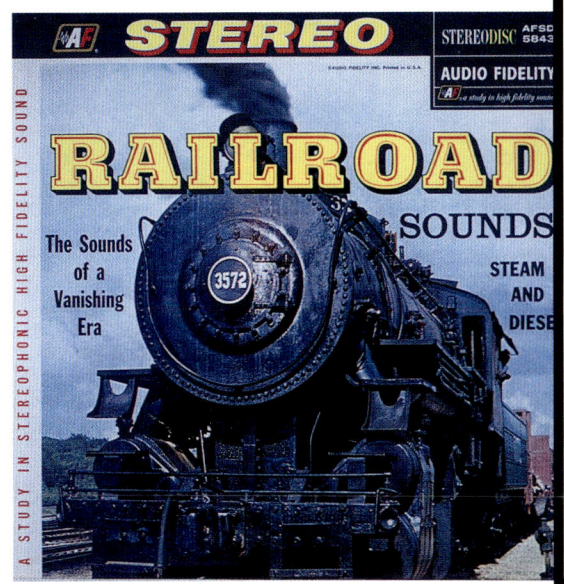

One of the first stereo records was Audio Fidelity's Railroad Sounds.
Railroad Sounds
Audio Fidelity, 1957

Giant Wurlitzer, Vol. 3
Leon Berry
Audio Fidelity, 1958

Hawaiian Percussion
Billy Mure
Strand, late 1950s

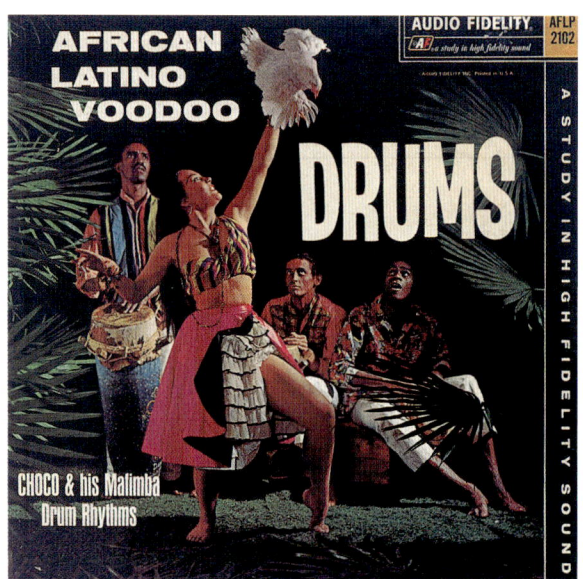

African Latino Voodoo Drums
Choco and His Mafimba Drum Rhythms
Audio Fidelity, 1963

Percussion Spectacular
Arthur Lyman
HiFi Records,
early 1960s
Cover design:
George Lieberman

Skin Tight
Marty Gold
RCA Victor, 1959

More of Other Worlds, Other Sounds
Esquivel and His Orchestra
Reprise Records, 1962
Cover: Norman Gollin
Art director: Merle Shore

Esquivel is a lucky man. He has won the Mexican lottery twice—once in the 1950s, $400,000; and again in the 1960s, $240,000.

Exploring New Sounds in Hi-Fi
Juan Garcia Esquivel
RCA Victor, 1959

Esquivel

The van Gogh of Space Age Pop was Mexico's Juan Garcia Esquivel, or simply Esquivel! Now deemed a genius by Space Age Pop aficionados, Esquivel took pop music beyond anything ever heard before, often by giving new, complex arrangements to familiar tunes.

Variety called him "the Mexican Duke Ellington," and some have deemed him the King of Space Age Pop.

Esquivel was born in Tampico, Mexico, in 1918. He taught himself the piano, and by fourteen was a soloist on a popular Mexico City radio station. By eighteen, he was arranging, conducting, and composing his own five-vocalist, twenty-two-piece band. He became immensely popular in Mexico, and in 1957, he looked north and signed with RCA Victor.

Esquivel arrived in America just as stereo was blossoming. His compositions deluged the listener with instruments and effects never heard before, much less on the same song—piano, vibes, brass, percussion, and his trademark slide guitar; and a chorus of "pow!," a harpsichord "zing," and a "zu-zu-zu."

For *Other Worlds, Other Sounds*, his first American album, he was brought to RCA's Hollywood studio and given five hours of studio time to record. On the album, he arranged the instruments (a twenty-six-piece orchestra), vocals (the Van Horne Singers), and even played the piano.

Esquivel's American spokesman, producer and radio personality Irwin Chusid says, "The album's astonishing range of musical textures and moonscape cover art firmly staked his claim in the orchestral pop pantheon and established his unique persona."

For his 1962 recording *Latin-Esque*, Esquivel proved the consummate perfectionist. To attain the truest stereo sound for the album, he divided his orchestra in half and placed it in two studios in separate buildings, led by two conductors.

Through a complex system of intercommunication using headphones, the musicians were able to hear each other and play together just as if they were in the same room. But the sound clearly came from different channels.

After *Latin-Esque*, Esquivel left the studio for twelve years to play the Tahoe–Vegas circuit. In 1974 his orchestra broke up and Esquivel returned to Mexico.

In 1978 he recorded an album tied to the children's TV series *Burbujas*. He also composed the music for several American TV shows, including *The Tall Man*, *Charlie's Angels*, *Kojak*, and *Simon and Simon*. A large library of his incidental music can still be heard on television.

Today, a back injury keeps Esquivel confined to a wheelchair, but he says he continues to dream up new and exciting sounds.

The Artists

Leo Addeo
Hawaii in Hi-Fi
RCA Camden

Many Albam
More Double Exposure
RCA

Herb Alpert
Whipped Cream and Other Delights
A&M

Leroy Anderson
Leroy Anderson Conducts
Decca

Ray Anthony
Golden Horn
Capitol

Jan August
Music for the Quiet Hour
Mercury

Warren Barker
Hawaiian Eye
Warner Brothers

John Barry
James Bond film scores
United Artist

Sid Bass
From Another World
Vik

Les Baxter
Ritual of the Savage
Capitol

Stanley Black
Exotic Percussion
London

Harry Breuer
Mallet Mischief
Audio Fidelity

Jack Burger
The End of Bongos
HiFi Records

Al Caiola
Percussion and Guitars
Time, UA

Frankie Carle
At the Piano
Columbia

David Carroll
Let's Dance
Mercury

Otto Cesana
Ecstasy
Columbia

Frank Chacksfield
You
London

Frank Comstock
Music from Outer Space
Warner Brothers

Ray Conniff
'S Wonderful
Columbia

Don Costa
Music to Break a Sublease
ABC Paramount

Jack Costanzo
Latin Fever
Liberty

Xavier Cugat
Bread, Love and ChaChaCha
Columbia, Mercury

Lenny Dee
Dee-Lightful
Decca

Martin Denny
Exotica
Liberty

Leo Diamond
The Harmonica Magic of Leo Diamond
RCA Victor

Webley Edwards
Hawaiian Paradise
Capitol

Esquivel!
Latin-Esque
RCA

Percy Faith
South Pacific
Columbia

Ferrante & Teicher
Blast Off!
Westminster

Irving Fields
Live from the Emerald Room
Decca

Russ Garcia
Fantastica
Liberty

Jackie Gleason
Music, Martinis, and Memories
Capitol

Marty Gold
Skin Tight
RCA

Morton Gould
Jungle Drums
RCA

Bernie Green
Futura
RCA

The Harmonicats
Cat's Meow
Mercury

Richard Haymen
Reminiscing
Command

Dick Hyman Trio
The Age of Electronicus
Command

Henry Jerome
Brazen Brass
Decca

Horst Jankowski
The Genius of Jankowski
Mercury

Bert Kaempfert
That Happy Feeling
Decca

André Kostelanetz
Carnival Tropicana
Columbia

Thurston Knudson
Primitive Percussion
Reprise

Liberace
Mr. Showmanship!
Dot

Enoch Light
Persuasive Percussion
Command

Living Strings
Music of Hawaii
RCA Camden

Arthur Lyman
Exotica
HiFi Records

Richard Maltby
Hi-Fi Moods by Maltby
Vik

Henry Mancini
Peter Gunn
RCA

Mantovani
Romantic Melodies
London Records

The Markko Polo Adventurers
Orienta
RCA

Ray Martin
Dynamica
RCA

Robert Maxwell
Ebb Tide
Columbia

Billy May
Music for Uptight Guys
Capitol

Peter Nero
Hail the Conquering Nero
RCA

Melachrino Orchestra
Music for Daydreaming
RCA

Mitch Miller
Sing Along with Mitch
Columbia

Hugo Montenegro
Bongs and Brass
Time Records

Noro Morales
Mambo with Morales
Harmony

Tony Mottola
Guitar…USA
Command Records

Billy Mure
Super-Sonic Guitars
Strand

Korla Pandit
Hypnotique
Fantasy

Norrie Paramor
Jet Flight
Capitol

Les Paul and Mary Ford
Galloping Guitars
Capitol

Perrey and Kingsley
The In Sounds from Way Out!
Vanguard

André Popp (Elsa Popping)
Delirium in Hi-Fi
Columbia

Franck Pourcel
Les Baxter's La Femme
Capitol

Perez Prado
Havana 3 A.M.
RCA

Louis Prima
The Wildest
Capitol

Sid Ramin
New Thresholds in Sound
RCA

Henri René
Music for Bachelors
RCA

Nelson Riddle
Sea of Dreams
Capitol

Tito Rodriguez
Mambo Madness
Tico, United Artists

Edmundo Ros
Bongos from the South
London

David Rose
Concert with a Beat!
MGM

Pete Rugolo
Music for Hi-Fi Bugs
Mercury

Santo and Johnny
Sleep Walk
Canadian American

Sauter-Finegan
Inside Sauter-Finegan
RCA

Dick Schory
Runnin' Wild
RCA

George Shearing
Latin Escapade
Capitol

Tak Shindo
Brass and Bamboo
Capitol

Mike Simpson
Discussion in Percussion
Mercury

Felix Slatkin
The Fantastic Strings of Felix Slatkin
Liberty

Yma Sumac
Voice of the Xtabay
Capitol

Bob Thompson
On the Rocks
RCA

The Three Suns
Having a Ball with the Three Suns
RCA

Billy Vaughn
Sweet Music and Memories
Dot

Al Viola
Guitars
Liberty

Walter Wanderly
Rain Forest
Verve

Julius Wechter
Comin' in the Back Door
A&M

Lawrence Welk
Easy Listening
Coral, Dot

Ruth Welcome
Zither Magic
Capitol

Paul Weston
Music for Dreamtime
Capitol, Columbia

Roger Williams
Till
Kapp

Hugo Winterhalter
Hugo Winterhalter Goes…Latin
RCA

George Wright
Have Organ, Will Travel
HiFi Records

Discography

**Les Baxter
(Capitol unless noted otherwise)
1950 to 1960s**

Music out of the Moon
Thinking of You
The Passions
Perfume Set to Music, RCA
Arthur Murray Favorites: Tangos
Ritual of the Savage
Kaleidoscope
Tamboo!
Caribbean Moonlight
Skins! Bongo Party with Les Baxter
'Round the World with Les Baxter
Midnight on the Cliffs
Ports of Pleasure
Space Escapade
Selections from "South Pacific"
Wild Guitars
Confetti
Love Is a Fabulous Thing
African Jazz
Jungle Jazz
The Sacred Idol
Jewels of the Sea
Young Pops
Broadway '61
Sensational!
Sounds of Adventure
Voices in Rhythm, Reprise
The Primitive and the Passionate, Reprise
Soul of the Drums, Reprise
Academy Award Winners: 1963, Reprise
Les Baxter's Balladeers
Que Mango! (with 101 Strings), Alshire
Million-Seller Hits, Alshire
African Blue, Crescendo
Barbarian (soundtrack), American International
Alakazam the Great (soundtrack), Vee-Jay
Hell's Belles (soundtrack), Sidewalk
The Dunwich Horror (soundtrack), American International
Bora Bora (soundtrack), American International

**Xavier Cugat
Late 1940s to early 1960s**

Dance with Cugat, Columbia
Quiet Music, Columbia
Cugat's Favorite Rhumbas, Columbia
Ole!, Columbia
Cha-Cha-Cha, Columbia
Mambo at the Waldorf, Columbia
Merengue by Cugat, Columbia
Bread, Love and Cha Cha Cha, Columbia
Cugat Calvacade, Columbia
Waltzes—but by Cugat, Columbia
Cugat Spain, RCA Victor
That Latin Beat, RCA Camden
Spanish Eyes, Coral
Cugat's Favorites, Mercury
Mambo, Mercury
Cugat Caricatures, Mercury
Plays the Music of Ernesto Lecuona, Mercury
Viva Cugat!, Mercury
The Best of Cugat, Mercury
Plays Continental Hits, Mercury
Dance Party, Decca
The Best of Xavier Cugat, MCA

**Martin Denny
Liberty
1950s and 1960s**

Exotica
Exotica, Volume II

Forbidden Island
Primitiva
Hypnotique
Afro-Desia
Exotica, Volume III
Quiet Village
The Enchanted Sea
Exotic Sounds from the Silver Screen
A Taste of India
A Taste of Honey
Mondo Cane
Hawaiian Tattoo
Spanish Village
Exotic Sounds Visits Broadway
Exotic Percussion
Exotic Suite
Exotique Moog

Juan Garcia Esquivel
(RCA unless noted otherwise)
1950s and 1960s

To Love Again
Other Worlds, Other Sounds
Four Corners of the World
Exploring New Sounds in Hi-Fi
Exploring New Sounds in Stereo
Strings Aflame
Infinity in Sound
Infinity in Sound, Volume 2
Latin-Esque
More of Other Worlds, Other Sounds, Reprise

Ferrante & Teicher
Prepared Piano Works
1950s and 1960s

Soundproof, Westminster
Heavenly Sounds in Hi-Fi, ABC Paramount
Postcards from Paris
Ferrante & Teicher with Percussion, ABC Paramount
Adventures in Carols, Westminster
Xmas Hi–Favorites
Blast Off!, ABC Paramount
Themes from Broadway Shows, ABC Paramount
Hi-Fireworks, Columbia
Dynamic Twin Pianos, United Artists

Jackie Gleason
Capitol
1950s and 1960s

Music for Lovers Only
Lover's Rhapsody
Music to Make You Misty
Tawny
Lonesome Echo
Music, Martinis and Memories
Romantic Jazz
Music to Remember Her
Music to Change Her Mind
Night Winds
Music for the Love Hours
Velvet Brass
Jackie Gleason Presents Oooo!
The Torch with the Blue Flame
Riff Jazz
Aphrodesia
The Gentle Touch

Richard Haymen
(Mercury unless noted otherwise)
1950s and 1960s

Reminiscing
Love Is a Many Splendored Thing
Come with Me to Far-Away Places
My Fair Lady
Only Memories

Great Motion Picture Themes of Victor
   Young
Voodoo!
Havana in Hi-Fi
Campfire Songs
Harmonica Holiday
Conducts Pop Concert in Sound
Let's Get Together
Cinematic, Command
Genuine Electric Latin Love Machine,
   Command

**Enoch Light
Command and Project 3
1950s and 1960s**
Command Releases:
Persuasive Percussion
Provocative Percussion
Million Dollar Sound of the World's Most
   Precious Violins
The Million Dollar Sound of the World's
   Most Precious Violins, Volume 2
The Private Life of a Private Eye
Provocative Percussion, Volume 2
Bongos/Flute/Guitars
Pertinent Percussion Cha-Chas

Persuasive Percussion, Volume 3
Big Bold and Brassy
Reeds and Percussion
Provocative Percussion, Volume 3
Far Away Places
Stereo 35/MM
Persuasive Percussion, Volume 4
Stereo 35/MM, Volume 2
Provocative Percussion, Volume 4
Enoch Light & His Orchestra at Carnegie
   Hall Play Irving Berlin
Big Band Bossa Nova
Far Away Places, Volume 2
Let's Dance the Bossa Nova
1963: The Year's Most Popular Themes
Rome
Dimension 3
Great Themes from Hit Films
Discotheque Dance, Dance, Dance
Discotheque, Volume 2
Persuasive Percussion: 1966
Musical Explorations in Sound
Project 3 Releases:
Enoch Light's Action
Spaced Out
Permissive Polyphonic

The Big Band Hits of the 40s
Big Hits of the 20s
Charge!
The Big Band Hits of the 40s and 50s
Future Sound Shock

**Julie London
Liberty
1950s and 1960s**
Julie Is Her Name
Lonely Girl
Calender Girl
About the Blues
Make Love to Me
Julie
Julie Is Her Name, Volume 2
London by Night
Swing Me an Old Song
Your Number Please
Julie…at Home
Around Midnight
Send for Me
Whatever Julie Wants
Sophisticated Lady
Love Letters
Love on the Rocks

Latin in a Satin Mood
The End of the World
The Wonderful World of Julie London
Julie London
Our Fair Lady
Feeling Good
All Through the Night
For the Night People
Nice Girls Don't Stay for Breakfast
With Body and Soul
Easy Does It

**Arthur Lyman
(HiFi and Life Records unless noted otherwise)
1950s and 1960s**
Leis of Jazz
Taboo
Hawaiian Sunset
Bwana A
Legend of Pele
Bahia
On Broadway
Taboo 2
Yellow Bird

Exotic Percussion
Colorful Percussion
Many Moods of Arthur Lyman
I Wish You Love
Cotton Fields
Blowin' in the Wind
Mele Kalikimaka
Isle of Enchantment
Call of the Midnight Sun
Hawaiian Sunset, Volume 2
Polynesia
Greatest Hits
Lyman '66
The Shadow of Your Smile
Aloha, Amigo
Il Ikai
At the Port of Los Angeles
Latitude
Aphrodesia
The Winners' Circle
Today's Greatest Hits
At the Crescendo, Crescendo
Paradise, Crescendo
Cast Your Fate to the Wind, Crescendo
Puka Shells, Crescendo

Authentic Hawaiian Favorites, Olympic Records

**Perez Prado
(RCA unless noted otherwise)
1950s to 1960**
Mambo Jambo, Crown
Mambo by the King
Mambo Mania
Voodoo Suite
Havana 3 A.M.
Latin Satin
Dance Rhythms, Diplomat
Mambo Happy
Perez
Dilo Ugh!
Pops and Prado
Big Hits by Prado
A Touch of Tabasco
Exotic Suite of the Americas
Rockambo
The New Dance La Chunga
The Twist Goes Latin: Exotic Suite

Our Man in Latin America
Dance Latino
Great Mambos, Bell
Latin Dance Party, Promenade
Perez Prado's Dance Party, Spinorama
Beautifully Yours, Springboard
And His Famous Latin Orchestra, Halo

Yma Sumac
1950s to 1970s

Voice of the Xtabay, Capitol
Flahooey, Capitol
Legend of the Sun Virgin, Capitol
Inca Taqui, Capitol
Mambo, Capitol
Legend of the Jivaro, Capitol
Fuego Del Andes, Capitol
Miracles, London

The Three Suns
(RCA unless noted otherwise)
1950 to early 1960s

Twilight Time, Varsity
Three-Quarter Time
Hands Across the Table
Twilight Moods
The Three Suns Present Busy Fingers
Christmas Party
Slumbertime
Pop Concert Favorites
Mods
Top Pops
Polka Time
Sacred Hymns
Soft and Sweet
Sounds of Christmas
My Reverie
Slumber Time
Malaguena
High Fi and Wide
Easy Listening
Midnight for Two
The Things I Love in Hi-Fi
Let's Dance with the Three Suns
Love in the Afternoon
Having a Ball with the Three Suns
Swingin' on a Star
A Ding Dong Daddy Christmas
Twilight Memories
On a Magic Carpet
Dancing on a Cloud
Fever and Smoke
Fun in the Sun
Movin' 'n' Groovin'
Warm and Tender

RCA's Stereo Action series
1961 and 1962

Dynamica, Ray Martin
It's Magic, Marty Gold
Runnin' Wild, Dick Schory
Sounds Terrific!, Ted Textor
Crazy Rhythm, Guitars Unlimited
Futura, Bernie Green
Stereo Action Goes Hollywood, Marty Gold
Stereo Action Goes Broadway, Dick Schory
Paradise Regained, Leo Addeo
Excitement, Incorporated, Ray Martin
Holiday for Percussion, Dick Schory
More Double Exposure, Manny Album
Dynamic Dimensions, Henri René
Stereo Action Unlimited, Various Artists
Latin-Esque, Esquivel

Selected Bibliography

Books

Baines, Anthony. *Oxford Companion to Musical Instruments*. London: Oxford University Press, 1992.

Clarke, Donald. *The Rise and Fall of Popular Music*. New York: St. Martin's Press, 1995.

Clarke, Donald. *The Penguin Encyclopedia of Popular Music*. New York: Penguin, 1989.

The Diagram Group. *Musical Instruments of the World*. New York: Facts On File, Inc., 1976.

Fox, Stephen. *The Mirror Makers: A History of American Advertising and Its Creators*. New York: William Morrow & Company, Inc., 1984.

Halberstam, David. *The Fifties*. New York: Ballantine Books, 1994.

Henry, William A., III. *The Great One: The Life and Legend of Jackie Gleason*. New York: Doubleday, 1992.

Hine, Thomas. *Populuxe*. New York: Alfred A. Knopf, 1986.

Jonas, Susan, and Marilyn Nissenson. *Going Going Gone: Vanishing Americana*. San Francisco: Chronicle Books, 1994.

Jones, Dylan. *Ultra Lounge: The Lexicon of Easy Listening*. New York: Universe Publishing, 1997.

Lanza, Joseph. *The Cocktail: The Influence of Spirits on the American Psyche*. New York: Picador, 1995.

———. *Elevator Music: A Surreal History of Muzak, Easy-Listening, and Other Moodsong*. New York: St. Martin's Press, 1994.

Manuel, Peter Lamarche. *Caribbean Currents*. Philadelphia: Temple University Press, 1995.

McCloud, Barry. *Definitive Country*. New York: Perigee, 1995.

Millard, Andre. *America on Record: A History of Recorded Sound*. New York: Cambridge University Press, 1995.

Moses, Robert, Alicia Potter, and Beth Rowen. *A&E Entertainment Almanac 1997: An Information Please Almanac*. Boston: Houghton Mifflin Company, 1996.

Osborne, Jerry. *Rockin' Records 17th Edition, 1995–1996*. Duboque, Iowa: Antique Trader Books, 1995.

Pendergast, Roy M. *Film Music: A Neglected Art*. New York: W. W. Norton & Company, 1977.

Sanjek, Russell. Updated by David Sanjek. *Pennies from Heaven: The American Popular Music Business in the Twentieth Century*. New York: Da Capo Press, 1988.

Scheur, Steven H. *Movies on TV, 1982-1983 Edition*. New York: Bantam, 1981.

Schwartz, Carol. *VideoHound's Complete Guide to Cult Flicks and Trash Pics.* Detroit: Visible Ink Press, 1996.

Stambler, Irwin. *The Encyclopedia of Pop, Rock and Soul.* New York: St. Martin's Press, 1989.

Umphred, Neal. *Goldmine's Price Guide to Collectible Record Albums.* Iola, Wisconsin: Krause Publications, 1994.

Vale, V. and Andrea Juno. *Incredibly Strange Music, Volume I and II.* San Francisco: RE/SEARCH Publications, 1994.

Weatherby, W. J. *Jackie Gleason: An Intimate Portrait of the Great One.* New York: Pharos Books, 1992.

Zelnik-Geldys, Suzanne. *ABCs of Ballroom Dance.* Dubuque, Iowa: Kendall/Hunt Publishing Company, 1991.

Articles

Chenault, Jeff. "Billy Mure: A Man and His Guitar." *Cool and Strange Music Magazine*, no. 5, 1997.

Ferrante, Art. "Prepared Piano Memories." *Cool and Strange Music Magazine*, no. 5, 1997.

Glenn, Joshua. "Cocktail Nation." *Cake*, vol.11, no. 22, 1994.

Heller, Steven. "For the Record." *Critique*, no. 7, 1998.

Hering, Ted. "A Brief History of Electronic Music." *Cool and Strange Music Magazine*, no. 4, 1997.

Kaz, Ed. "King Louis: The Louis Prima Story." *Cool and Strange Music Magazine*, no. 4, 1997.

Peek, R. Preston. "A Few Slices of Sleazecake." *Cool and Strange Music Magazine*, no. 4, 1997.

Powers, Jim. "Mondo Melodica Exotica." *Goldmine*, vol. 22, no. 9, April 26, 1996.

Rothenberg, Randall. "Welcome to…Cocktail Culture." *Esquire*, April 1997.

Rev. Susie the Floozie. "Music for Every Mood Swing." *Cool and Strange Music Magazine*, no. 10, 1998.

Websites

Dada'quariums Exotica. http://www.bewoner.dma.be/Dada

The Exotica Standards. http://www.netrail.net~bbigelow/homepage.htm

The Exotica Mailing List. exotica-request@xmission.com

Goldmine Online. http://www.Krause.com/goldmine/index.htm

Vik Trola's Lounge of Self Indulgence. chaoskitty.com/t chaos/lounge.htm

Quiet Village
Martin Denny
Scamp, 1997

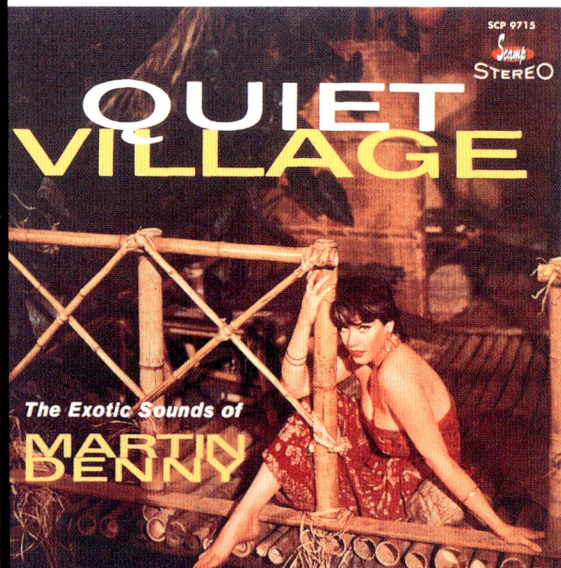

The Enchanted Sea
Martin Denny
Scamp, 1997

Record-Ordering Information

Most of the record labels featured in this book have re-released some fabulous Space Age Pop recordings. For information, please contact the following:

BMG/RCA Records
212-930-4000

Capitol Records
http://www.ultralounge.com
213-462-6252

Columbia Records
212-833-8000

The Curb Group
615-321-5080

DCC Compact Classics (Music for Bachelor's Den)
800-301-MUSIC (6874)

Del-Fi (Eden Ahbez)
P.O. Box 69188, Los Angeles, CA 90069
http://www.del-fi.com or email: info@delfi.com
800-99-DEL-FI

Dionysus (Robert Drasnin, Les Baxter)
Write for catalog: Dionysus Records, P.O. Box 1975, Burbank, CA 91507

HiFi/Rykodisc (Arthur Lyman and other HiFi artists)
http://www.rykodisc.com
email: hifi@rykodisc.com
888-2-EARFUL

Madacy Entertainment (101 Strings)
http://www.101strings.com

MCA Records
818-777-4000

Mercury Records
212-333-8000

Reprise Records
818-846-9090

Rhino Records
310-474-4778

Scamp (Martin Denny and 101 Strings)
http://www.caroline.com
Scamp, 104 West 29th Street, 4th Floor, New York, NY 10001

Vanguard Records (Perrey and Kingsley)
http://www.VanguardRecords.com

Varese Sarabande (Ferrante and Teicher, Roger Williams, and Dick Hyman)
800-VARESE-4

Warner Bros. Records
818-846-9090

Acknowledgments

Thanks to all the musicians and arrangers who created the mood-enhancing music discussed in this book.

And, of course, to all the photographers, artists, and designers who made the fantastic album cover art. And to Esme, with love.

Thanks:

Lenny Dee
Irwin Chusid
Joseph Holmes
Brad Bigelow
Joseph Lanza
Scott Smith
The Palm Beach County Library
The Salvation Army
Goodwill Industries
Goldmine
Madeleine Findley, Cal Morgan, Dana Albarella, and Bert Yaeger at St. Martin's Press
Cool And Strange Music Magazine
Space Age Bachelor Pad Website
Exotica Standards Website
Byron Werner
David Greenberg

Thanks also:

BMG/RCA Victor
Camden
Columbia
Command
Coral
Crown
Decca
Dot
EMI/Capitol
Grand Award
HiFi
Liberty
Madacy Entertainment
MCA
Mercury
Polygram
RCA Custom
Reprise
Rykodisc
Scamp
United Artists
Vanguard
Vik
Warner Brothers

Index

A&R (Artists and Repertoire) men, 14
Addeo, Leo, 45
album covers, 1, 15-17, 79
Audio Fidelity (record label), 3, 96, 99

Barron, Louis and Bebe, 88
Bass, Sid, 5, 89
Baxter, Les, 5, 39-41, 57
Belly dancing music and records, 72
Bongoson, 57

Camus, Amy, 41
Cha-Cha, 57, 59
Chacksfield, Frank, 23-24
Chanteuse, 76-77
Cheesecake covers, 79
Cocktail music (**Music for Sipping Martinis**), 74-85
cocktail pianist, 76
cocktail records, 77, 81
Columbia Records, 2
Command Records, 19, 97
Comstock, Frank, 89
concept album, 10
Conniff, Ray, 26
Cugat, Xavier, 55

Darian, Anita, 69
dances, 55-67, 59, 72
Dee, Lenny, v-ix, 76
Denny, Martin, 44, 69, 76
"Dilo," 56

Eastern instruments, 71
Eastern music (**The Exotic East**), 66 73
Ellington, Duke, 38
Esquivel, Juan Garcia, 6, 89, 101 103
Exotica instruments, 50
Exotica films, 47

Exotica songs, 59
Exotic sounds, motifs, 3

Exotica, 39-53
Exotica, 44

Fantasia, 95
Ferrante and Teicher, 5, 26, 89
Fields, Irving, 76
Films, 87, 88, 92
Forbidden Planet, 88
45-rpm, 2
Frey, Sidney, 96

Gatefold, 19, 97
Gleason, Jackie, 5, 77, 79
Grand Award, 19
gypsy music, 69

Hawaiian music, 44, 45
Haymen, Richard, 43
Hi-Fidelity, 2
instruments, 50, 71
Jasmine and Jade, 67
Jungle and Tiki films, 47
Jungle Exotica, 39-53

Kostelanetz, André, 24, 57

Lane, Abbe, 76, 79
Latin Invasion, The, 55-65
Latin records, 62
Latin sounds, 57-58
Lecuona, Ernesto: songs, 60
Lecuona, Ernesto, 58, 60
Lecuona, Margarita, 60
Light, Enoch, 6, 19, 97
London, Julie, 76-77, 78-79
Los Indios Tabajaras, 58
lounge acts, 75-76
LP (long-playing record) (**The LP and New Frontiers**), 1-9

Lyman, Arthur, 44, 76, 98

Mambo madness, 56-57
Mambo, 55-57, 59
Mantovani, Annunzio, 3, 23, 34
Maria Elena, "Maria Elena," 58
Markko Polo and the Adventurers, 68,98
Miller, Dick, 24
Miller, Mitch, 14
Mood music (**Music for Gracious Living**), 21-37
Mood series, 22-23
Moog synthesizer, 90
Moog, Robert, 90
Murray, Arthur, 55
Music for Gracious Living, 3, 21

101 Strings, 24, 35-37
Orienta, 68

Pandit, Korla, 69
Paul, Les and Mary Ford, 88
Perrey and Kingsley, 90
Polynesia, 3
Polynesian music, 44, 45
Popp, André, 88
Prado, Perez, 55-56, 57
Prima, Louis, 75-76
Project 3, 19
Provocative and Persuasive Percussion series, 97
Puente, Tito, 56, 57

"Quiet Village," 41, 44

Ritual of the Savage, 10, 39-41
Rockambo, 57
Rodriguez, Tito, 56-57
Rumba, 59

Sacred Idol, 57

Scott, Raymond, 89
78-rpm, 2
Shindo, Tak, 68
Siday, Eric, 89
Sing Along with Mitch series, 14
Smith, Keely, 76
Sodsai, Sondi, 68-69
Soundproof, 89
Space Age Pop album covers, 15-17
Space Age Pop models, 16
Space Age Pop music, 1
Space Age Pop musicians, 5
Space Age Pop songs, 6, 11, 13
Space films, 92
Space music (**The Sounds of Space**), 86-93
Spellbound, 88
Stereo Action (RCA), 6, 97
stereo (**And Then There Was Stereo**), 95-102
stereophonic, 2
Stordahl, Axel, 67, 68
Suburbia (Mood Music), 3
Sumac, Yma, 41-43
Supermarket music, 26
Suzuki, Pat, 68
synthesizer, 88

Taboo, 44
Theremin, 88
Theremin, Leon, 88
35-millimeter tape, 97
33⅓ rpm, 2,3
Three Suns, The, 79
Tiki Exotica, 44-53

vinyl archaeologists, 1
vinyl, vinylite, 2

Warren, Ernie, 45
Weston, Paul, 21
Westrex, 95, 96

Album Covers Index

Addeo, Leo: *Hawaii in Hi-Fi*, 53
Aloma, Hal: *Lure of the Islands*, 52

Barclay, Peter: *Music for Gracious Living: Do-It-Yourself*, 20; *Foursome*, 24
Bass, Sid: *From Another World*, 86
Baxter, Les: *Ritual of the Savage*, 40
Be There at 5: Conversational Music for Cocktails, 84
Berry, Leon: *Giant Wurlitzer, Vol. 3*, 99
Bowen, Hill: *I Married an Angel*, 31
Bud Dant, Charles: *The 50th State*, 51

Carroll, David: *Let's Dance*, 12
Chacksfield, Frank: *Waltzes to Remember*, 29
Choco and His Mafimba Drum Rhythms: *African Latino Voodoo Drums*, 100
Christian, Bobby: *Strings for a Space Age*, 91
Conniff, Ray: *'S Awful Nice*, 27
Cugat, Xavier: *The Best of Xavier Cugat*, 80; *Cugat Plays Continental Hits*, 98
Cwanda Group, The: *Taboo*, 45

Darian, Anita: *East of the Sun*, 70
Dee, Lenny: *Down South*, vi; *Dee-Lirious*, ix
Denny, Martin: *Primitiva*, 7; *Exotica*, 38; *Quiet Village*, 114; *Enchanted Sea*, 114

El-Bakkar, Mohammed: *Port Said: Music of the Middle East*, 72
El-Safi, Wadih and Najah Salam: *I Remember Lebanon*, 73
Esquivel, Juan Garcia: *Other Worlds, Other Sounds*, 9; *More of Other Worlds, Other Sounds*, 102; *Exploring New Sounds in Hi-Fi*, 102

Faith, Percy: *Swing Low in Hi Fi: Spirituals for Orchestra*, 30
Faz, Roberto: *Faz*, 62
Feijoo, Marcel: *Continental Tangos*, 64
Ferrante and Teicher: *Blast Off!*, 8; *The Enchanted Ferrante and Teicher*, 28; *Soundproof*, 88
Font, Ralph: *Tabu*, 17

Garcia, Pedro: *Tropical Cruise*, 48; *A Tropical Affair*, 48
Gleason, Jackie: *Jackie Gleason Presents Oooo!*, 77
Gold, Marty: *Skin Tight*, 100

Harkness, David: *Hammond Organ in Hi-Fi*, 18
Harmonicats, Jerry Murad's: *The Cat's Meow*, 5
Haymen, Richard: *Voodoo!*, 44
Hollywood Playboys Orchestra: *Music for Playboys to Play By*, 82
Hyman, Dick: *The Age of Electronicus*, 93

Kaempfert, Bert: *That Happy Feeling*, 31
King, Pete: *The Sensuous Music of Pete King*, 3
Kostelanetz, André: *Lure of the Tropics*, 30; *Carnival Tropicana*, 62

Latin Fire, 54
Lecuona, Ernesto: *Lecuona's Music in Dance Tempos*, 60
LeMar, Eddie: *Businessman's Bounce: Music for the Expense Account Set*, 82
Light, Enoch: *Provocative Percussion*, 18; *Guitar Underground*, 19; *Provocative Percussion, Vol. III*, 104
London, Julie: *Julie London*, 78
Los Indios Tabajaras: *Maria Elena*, 58
Los Rumberos de Cuba: *Rumba on a Cloud*, 65
Lupa, Guy: *The Esquire Album of Music for the Continental Host*, 74
Lyman, Arthur: *Taboo*, 4; *Taboo Vol. 2*, 41; *Bahia*, 46; *Percussion Spectacular*, 101

Mambo in Havana, 65
Mantovani, Annunzio: *Romantic Melodies*, 34
Markko Polo Adventurers: *Orienta*, 66
Melachrino Strings, The: *Music for Dining*, 32; *Music for Reading*, 32; *Music for Daydreaming*, 33
Melis, José: *Latin American Stylings*, 63
Mure, Billy: *Hawaiian Percussion*, 100

101 Strings: *The 101 Strings Play the Best American Waltzes*, 36; *East of Suez*, 36; *Gypsy Campfires*, 37; *Sugar and Spice*, 37

Perrey, Jean Jacques: *The Amazing New Electronic Pop Sound of Jean Jacques Perrey*, 93
Perrey and Kingsley: *The In Sound from Way Out*, 90
Pike, Dave: *Manhattan Latin*, 63
Pincus, Paul: *Happy Occasions*, 27
Pourcel, Frank: *Les Baxter's La Femme*, x
Prado, Perez: *Mambo Jambo*, 56
Prado, Pupi: *Cha Cha Cha for Swingin Partners*, 64
Puente, Tito: *Cha Cha Cha's for Lovers*, 61

Railroad Sounds, 99
Rains, Gene: *Lotus Land*, 52
René, Henri: *Dynamic Dimensions*, 96
Riddle, Nelson: *Sea of Dreams*, 81

Sodsai, Sondi: *Sondi*, 68
Stewart, Danny: *Dance the Hula in the Moonlight*, 53
Stordahl, Axel: *Jasmine and Jade*, 70
Sumac, Yma: *Voice of the Xtabay*, 42
Surfmen, The: *The Sounds of Exotic Island*, 46

Three Suns, The: *Fever & Smoke*, 83; *Cocktail Time*, 85

Vaughn, Billy: *Sweet Music and Memories...*, 25

Welk, Lawrence: *Champagne Dancing Party*, 81
Weston, Paul: *Dreamtime Music by Paul Weston*, 22
Williams, Roger: *Mr. Piano*, 84

Young, Victor: *After Dinner Music*, 2